WINNING FLORIDA

How the Bush Team Fought the Battle

The Hoover Institution
gratefully acknowledges generous support from

TAD AND DIANNE TAUBE
TAUBE FAMILY FOUNDATION
KORET FOUNDATION

Founders of the program on
American Institutions and Economic Performance

and Cornerstone gifts from

SARAH SCAIFE FOUNDATION

WINNING FLORIDA

|||||||||||||||||||||||||||||||||||||||||||||||||||

How the Bush Team Fought the Battle

Robert Zelnick

HOOVER INSTITUTION PRESS
Stanford University **I** Stanford, California

The Hoover Institution on War, Revolution and Peace, founded at Stanford University in 1919 by Herbert Hoover, who went on to become the thirty-first president of the United States, is an interdisciplinary research center for advanced study on domestic and international affairs. The views expressed in its publications are entirely those of the authors and do not necessarily reflect the views of the staff, officers, or Board of Overseers of the Hoover Institution.

www.hoover.org

Hoover Institution Press Publication No. 500

First printing 2001

07 06 05 04 03 02 01 00   9 8 7 6 5 4 3 2 1

Manufactured in the United States of America

The paper used in this publication meets the minimum requirements of the American National Standard for Information Sciences—Permanence of Paper for Printed Library Materials, ANSI Z39.48–1984.

Library of Congress Cataloging-in-Publication Data

(Application for CIP data has been filed with the Library of Congress.)

ISBN 0-8179-2882-0

Contents

Acknowledgments

I should like to extend my deepest gratitude to John Raisian, Director of the Hoover Institution, for his confidence and generosity in supporting this project. Florida was flooded with reporters during the Bush-Gore post-election battle, and it has been flooded since then with authors. Despite the crowd, my thinking was that there was a good short book to be written about the strategy and tactics of the side that ultimately prevailed in a battle that was like playing chess to a metronome. Whether I was right, the reader can judge. But without John's support, there would have been no project.

Thanks also to Associate Director Richard Sousa, who was always reachable, and always prompt to provide needed assistance.

I am grateful for the work of Patricia Baker, Executive Editor of the Hoover Press, and the staff at Publication Services in Champaign, Illinois, for highly professional editing under a rigorous deadline.

My daughter Eva, an associate producer with Fox News in Washington, and my daughter Marni, who graduated this past June from Dartmouth, provided both quick and professional research assistance. Maybe sending them to college wasn't such a bad idea after all.

Megan Cooley, one of my graduate students at Boston University, also provided research assistance, also under difficult deadline pressure, and at a time when she was a bit under the weather. I am deeply appreciative of her efforts.

Many of the lawyers, and a few normal people, who fought gallantly in Florida, gave freely of their time in sharing their recollections with me and enlightening me as to how the various Florida operations meshed, and sometimes mashed. There are too many to mention by name, but some will be obvious to the reader.

Because the thrust of this study was on the internal deliberations of the Bush strategists in Florida, I spent relatively little time with those on the other side. I would, however, like to extend my appreciation to John Hardin Young, a senior Gore operator and coauthor of *The Recount Primer,* a key instructional manual for the Gore forces. Mr. Young offered some candid comments when we spoke and also sent a copy of his hard-to-get primer.

Thanks also to Senator Joseph Lieberman, a man I have admired for years, who is justifiably held in the highest regard by those who know him best. We had an interesting chat about the campaign during a business trip to Europe, and I much look forward to his comments about this book.

Finally, my most sincere thanks to my Boston University students for putting up with their professor, who spent most of the past semester crashing on this project while carrying the traditional three-course schedule. I hope my evaluations didn't suffer. And it is to them that I should like to dedicate this book.

CHAPTER I

Drawing the Battle Lines

Like most political intimates of George W. Bush, Ben Ginsberg, the general counsel of the Bush campaign, shared the pendulum-like swings of election night emotion in Austin, Texas. First came the tears as the three key battleground states—Michigan, Pennsylvania, and Florida—all seemed to fall into the Gore column. Then came the hope as Randy Enright, perhaps the soundest GOP consultant in Florida, and state chairman Al Cardenas assured the Austin people that the networks were wrong, and the state was still in play. Then that huge collective sigh of relief as the news organizations acknowledged their mistake and put Florida back into the "too close to call" category. Then the celebratory shouts, the hugs and high fives as the networks declared Bush the winner. The concession phone call from Gore. The drive to the capitol for the declaration of victory.

Ginsberg, who early in his professional life worked as a reporter in western Massachusetts, and now puts bread on the table by lobbying and lawyering with the well-wired Patton Boggs firm in Washington, never quite made it to the capitol that night. En route came the phone call from headquarters telling the motorcade that Florida was again "too close to call" and that Gore had phoned Bush a second time, now to withdraw his concession. Ginsberg abandoned the procession and headed back to Bush campaign headquarters to check the latest Florida figures. Bush still led by nearly two thousand votes, this time with nearly everything counted that could be counted on election night. Several thousand absentee ballots, most from overseas military personnel, would dribble in during the next ten days, but that was good; they were expected to add to the Bush margin. Regardless, Bush could still theoretically lose Florida yet still win the election if he managed to sweep Iowa, Wisconsin, New Mexico, and Oregon—the remaining states still up for grabs. But he was trailing in at least three of those states, so that prospect was dim. The good news: the arithmetic precluded a Gore victory without Florida regardless of what he won elsewhere.

Around 4:15 A.M., with Bush still clinging to his slim Florida lead, Ginsberg was approached by Don Evans, the chairman of Bush's campaign. "I suppose there will be a recount now," he said.

"Yeah, it's automatic with these numbers," Ginsberg replied. In Florida, any contest where the final margin does not exceed one half of one percent is subject to an automatic machine recount.

"Well, you better get down there," said Evans.

By 10:00 A.M. November 8, Ginsberg was airborne en route to Tallahassee. He was not particularly concerned about the recount ahead. After dwindling in the early morning hours, the Bush lead had stabilized and now stood at 1,784. Moreover, after years as a counsel in political races, Ginsberg had developed a rule of thumb for recounts: "The good gets better and the bad gets worse." Rarely had he seen results reversed on the basis of a recount. Usually leads were stretched. Of course, the recount he had in mind was the automatic machine recount demanded by Florida law. He was not at this point familiar with much else. Unlike the Gore camp, which before election day had assembled a series of legal "SWAT" teams poised to slash their way into the post-election battle in pivotal states, the Bush team had delegated to the Republican National Committee the task of assembling and learning the recount laws of all fifty states. There had been an RNC meeting on the subject, but the focus had been on races for the House of Representatives. A presidential recount was unprecedented, unforeseen, and unplanned for.

One could have forgiven Ginsberg a mild sense of déjà vu as he headed for Florida. Back in 1988 as a young counsel for the Republican National Committee, he had watched the Voter News Service, which was jointly owned at the time by the three major networks, AP, and UPI, use its exit polls to project Democrat Buddy MacKay the winner over Republican, Connie Mack, in their race for the United States Senate. ABC and CBS quickly followed suit. Overnight, however, Mack forged ahead and held on to win the seat. MacKay complained bitterly about undervotes. In four populous counties—Dade, Hillsborough, Palm Beach, and Sarasota—where he was thought to be leading, some 200,000 fewer votes had been cast in the Senate race than in the Bush-Dukakis presidential contest. MacKay demanded a manual recount in those four counties. Three declined, having found some evidence of machine malfunctions but none of fraud at a time when Florida law contained no provision for recounts triggered by an error in vote tabulation. Then, when a recount in Palm Beach County showed no material gain by MacKay as the recount progressed, the Democrat conceded and Mack took the seat.

In the battle for the presidency in 2000, however, Ginsberg would witness no such speedy resolution. Rather, he was flying into the heart of a Democratic free-fire zone designed to delegitimize the narrow Bush victory in Florida and overturn the results of the contest, thus making Al Gore and not George Bush the forty-third president of the United States. The elements of this strategy had already begun to take shape with complaints about an "illegal" ballot in Palm Beach County that had allegedly entrapped thousands of Gore supporters into casting their votes for the Independent

Party candidate, Patrick Buchanan. The principal elements of the Democratic strategy were:

1. Establish the moral basis for the effort by emphasizing the Gore-Lieberman victory in the popular vote

2. Promote the claim that large numbers of Floridians had been disenfranchised for reasons that ranged from faulty voting machines to racism

3. Play for time both with the public and the Democratic party by claiming that what the strategy is really defending is the right of all citizens to vote and to have their votes counted

4. Demand manual recounts employing the most flexible methods, in the most favorable jurisdictions

5. Attack the election results in the courts, directly where consistent with what became the "count all votes" mantra, and through allies and surrogates where direct involvement carries political liability

6. Try to make the liberal, activist Democratic Florida Supreme Court the ultimate arbiter of the Florida vote

On Wednesday morning Gore announced that he was sending William Daley, his campaign chairman, and former Secretary of State Warren Christopher to represent his interests in Florida. Daley, the son of one Chicago mayor and brother of another, had never provided evidence of having inherited his fair share of the family political genes. Christopher, dour and humorless, had spent much of his life handling sensitive political tasks, and choosing him seemed to be like choosing someone "above politics." For example, as Deputy Secretary of State in the Carter Administration, Christopher had been tapped to negotiate the release of the U.S. hostages held by Iran. More recently, as head of a reform commission, he had waded through the mess of the Los Angeles Police Department without ever muddying his cordovans.

"Because of what is at stake, this matter must be resolved expeditiously, but deliberately and without any rush to judgment," said Gore.[1]

Daley combined several "talking points" into a single response to a reporter's question as to whether he thought Gore had won the election: "There's no question he's ahead in the popular vote and ahead in the electoral vote. There is one state left to be decided. We believe, when those votes are counted and that process is complete, totally complete, Al Gore will have won the Electoral College and the popular vote and therefore will be the next president."[2]

The Bush team had its own former Secretary of State in the wings, James A. Baker, III. A shrewd Texan who had been the longtime friend and political strategist of former President George H. W. Bush, Baker had served as President Ronald Reagan's Chief of Staff before swapping jobs with Donald Regan to become Secretary of the Treasury in the second Reagan term. Later, as Bush's Secretary of State, he had helped persuade his Soviet counterpart, Edward Shevardnadze, to accept both the breakup of the Soviet Empire and the inclusion of a reunited Germany in NATO. He had also helped knit together the thirty-eight-state international coalition that expelled Iraq from Kuwait in the Persian Gulf War. But Baker's stint in Washington had ended unhappily when, responding to an eleventh-hour plea from Bush, he had taken over the President's faltering 1992 campaign, only to find it beyond resuscitation. Coming to the White House with four protégés—Margaret Tutwiler, Robert Zoellick, Janet Mullins, and Dennis Ross—Baker did little to disguise the fact that he resented having been forced to give up his job as the nation's top diplomat to take over a campaign from the incompetents who had been running it. White House staffers and those who had been part of the Bush campaign resented this sort of treatment from the "gang of five." They circulated word of how they stuck to themselves, even at the White House mess, never missing an opportunity to bad-mouth the way the campaign had been run before they got there. No one could pretend that the campaign had been run like a well-oiled machine, but with H. Ross Perot feeding off the normal Republican base and the economy barely arousing itself from recession, 1992 was a tough year, particularly with a man who made a better President than candidate.

Rumors that Baker had fallen out of favor with the Bush family, particularly former First Lady Barbara Bush, were probably false. After all, among the plans he abandoned to come to Florida was a hunting excursion with the former President and Prince Bandar, the Saudi Arabian Ambassador to Washington. Now an extremely fit seventy, Baker would impress both new and veteran members of the Bush team with his coolness under fire, the soundness of his political instincts, and his ability, shared with great quarterbacks, to see a situation developing over the entire field of play. "This campaign made a number of calls in Florida, none of them inevitable, all of them hotly debated at the time, and, in the end, virtually all of them right," recalled Kenneth Juster, a savvy Washington lawyer who worked in Florida through nearly all the thirty-six-day battle. "And Jim Baker was right every time."

"He can see around corners," said an admiring Margaret Tutwiler, who along with Zoellick joined Baker in Florida a day after the vote for what would prove a happier reunion than 1992. Ross, the remaining veteran of the unsuccessful 1992 political rescue mission, now running the Mideast peace effort from the State Department, would devote his energy this time around to sifting through the wreckage of the final Clinton initiative, hoping to leave the next president, regardless of identity, with something to work with.

Within 48 hours of his arrival, Baker, his longtime colleagues, and Ginsberg had put together the principal elements of a strategy to counter the Gore effort. Like Gore's strategy, it had both legal and political elements. The principal ones:

1. Claim the election was over, that Bush had won, and that the public interest demanded "finality."

2. Try to stop the counting, using the courts as the party of first resort, and if that fails, by urging strict interpretation of Florida statutory law.

3. Fight the "ground war" in the recount jurisdictions to limit the discretion of canvassing boards to find new votes in ballots rejected by voting machines.

4. Use the constitutionally mandated "plenary power" of the Republican-dominated legislature to determine how presidential electors are selected to offset the Democratic advantage among the vote counters and with the Florida Supreme Court.

5. Do not fall behind in the vote count.

6. Try to make the conservative Republican United States Supreme Court the ultimate arbiter of the Florida vote.

By the evening of November 8, Baker and Ginsberg had joined forces in Tallahassee, and both had met with the governor and his top political strategists to get a sense of where things stood. Governor Jeb Bush had earlier in the day recused himself form direct involvement in trying to sort out the Florida result, but he had already nailed down the services of the state's top election dispute lawyer, Barry Richard, of the Tallahassee firm of Greenberg Traurig. Moreover, his acting counsel, Frank Jimenez, had made certain that none of the state's top law firms would be hiring out to the Gore camp. The first day of the recount had gone uneventfully; Gore had picked up a total of eight votes, no danger signs there. Jimenez, State GOP Chairman Al Cardenas, and consultant Randy Enright had done their best to get GOP representatives to as many counting centers as possible. They found some of their best workers AWOL, having already departed on preplanned vacations. But they still managed to get warm bodies to about two-thirds of the centers. The Bush team needed all the local help it could get. The Gore campaign plane had flown seventy-two people into the state, and trial lawyers nationwide were being asked to volunteer for service in Florida. The Bush team, anticipating a two- or three-day electronic recount, numbered no more than a dozen outsiders.

The biggest furor seemed to be taking place over the so-called butterfly ballots of Palm Beach County. Designed by County Election Supervisor Teresa LePore to provide lettering large enough for the nearsighted elderly to read, the ballots presented candidates listed alternately on both sides of the ballot with punch holes running down the center. Gore's name was listed second on the left side of the ballot, but his punch hole was the third one down, just below that of Patrick Buchanan, whose name was on the right side. Despite large arrows directing voters to the appropriate holes, a number of voters apparently intending to vote for Gore may have mistakenly punched the Buchanan hole. Controversy over the confusing ballot had begun before noon. LePore's office had been asked by anxious party officials at midday to make certain the complexities were being explained in each precinct. Still, Buchanan received 3,411 votes in Palm Beach county, more than three times his total of 1,013 in Pinellas county, his second-best showing in the state.

By November 8, the first of the lawsuits by Gore supporters challenging the ballots and seeking a revote had been filed. Two days later, Daley told reporters that "our legal team has concluded that the ballot in Palm Beach County was unlawful."[3] In Washington, Gore's press secretary, Chris Lehane, suggested that when a similar problem had arisen in Tampa, the courts "took a statistical analysis of what the voting patterns had been throughout that city for a particular district . . . and they then took that statistical measure and applied it to that district."[4] In fact, no such remedy had ever been applied by the Florida courts absent a showing of massive fraud.

Bush's Florida election law specialists were certain that no challenge to the Palm Beach County ballots would be sustained. First, the design appeared to comply with Florida law. Second, a full description had been circulated to and approved by representatives of both political parties as well as the Secretary of State in advance of election day.

Additionally, a 1974 ruling by the Second District Florida Court of Appeals in *Nelson v. Robinson* had established unambiguous precedent to the effect that mere confusion engendered by the ballot design "does not amount to an impediment to the voters' free choice if reasonable time and study will sort it out. . . ."[5] In *Nelson,* the large number of offices and questions on the ballot had led officials to list certain candidates on a line under the one identifying the race and listing several candidates for it.

Furthermore, even had that judicial hurdle been surmounted, Gore's butterfly ballot case was doomed by the nonexistence of any appropriate remedy. That a court would simply apportion some unspecified number of votes along the lines of votes cast was unthinkable. And a revote was constitutionally impermissible. The United States Constitution provides that "the Congress may determine the time of choosing electors, and the day on which they shall give their vote; which day shall be the same throughout the United States" (Article 2, Section 1, clause 4). Accepting that authority, Congress passed 3 U.S.C.A. Section 1, which provides that "the electors of President and Vice President shall be appointed, in each State, on the Tuesday next after the first Monday in November in every fourth year succeeding every election of a President and Vice President." That day—November 7, 2000—already having come and gone, the courts were powerless to impose a date of their own choosing.

Legal remedies aside, Bush's Austin advisors felt that Gore was scoring some political points with the butterfly ballot dispute. Jesse Jackson was already in Florida beginning to kick up a fuss and others were on the way. To counter that ruckus, Evans organized a press briefing on November 9 at which Bush's political mastermind, Carl Rove, suggested that rather than ballot confusion, the Buchanan showing was the product of hard work. "Not that we're defending Pat Buchanan, but to set the record straight, there are 16,695 voters in Palm Beach county who registered as members of the Independent Party, the Reform Party or the American Reform Party, which were the labels borne this year by the reform effort in Florida."[6] Rove noted that the registration for these parties had increased by 110 percent since 1996, compared to 38 percent in the rest of Florida. Neighboring Broward County, for example, had only 476 voters registered in one of the three independent parties. Rove might have added that local factors similar to Palm Beach County's vote for Buchanan happened elsewhere even without the butterfly ballot. In Volusia County, for example, Libertarian Party Candidate Harry Browne received 3,211 votes—five times his best showing in any comparable county.

So Rove certainly had a point, even if Buchanan's savage fight for the Reform Party nomination had cost him dearly with party members and his forlorn, embittered campaign had pushed him practically off the charts from coast to coast. But Buchanan himself had already undermined Rove's argument by conceding to reporters that his showing in Palm Beach county was inflated and undoubtedly included the votes of many intending to cast their ballots for Gore.

Baker was not happy with the way Bush's Austin advisors had handled the issue. Trying to persuade the country that Pat Buchanan had surged in Palm Beach County was a tough sell. The basic message was that under Florida law the ballot was perfectly legal, and even if it wasn't, the time for Gore to protest was before the vote. Making a scene now was an act of political gamesmanship.

From this point on, Austin would generally defer to Tallahassee on the handling of Florida issues. On November 10 Baker took the opportunity in a statement to the press to address the butterfly ballot controversy in his own way: "There is a rule of law to be followed for elections. The state of Florida has established legal procedures to design, approve, publish, and if need be, to protest ballots before the election. A Democratic election supervisor designed the ballot. She approved it. The Democratic Party did not question it before the election. This butterfly-type ballot was used in recent elections in the same county under the same rules. Again, the Democrats did not complain. The overwhelming majority of voters who used the ballot understood it and cast valid votes. Our lawyers have confirmed the legality of this ballot and we have copies of the relevant Florida statute available for you to see."

Austin agreed that Florida, as the venue of the contest, should also be the venue of the principal public relations operation. Henceforth, the daily conference call would continue, as would the hundreds of daily calls between the two Bush operations. Baker was wary of using himself up during the first few days of battle, as Daley and Christopher had, in his view. Before long, visiting Republicans like Governor Marc Racicot of Montana, former senator Bob Dole, and New Jersey Governor Christie Todd Whitman would hold forth with reporters. Austin would complain that Baker did not maintain a forceful public presence in the state. But he would resist pressure from afar to get too deeply into the daily political savagery.

Baker had far more immediate concerns than butterfly ballots. Rather than confirming or even expanding Bush's election night lead, the electronic recount was producing something of a meltdown. The net gain for Gore in Duval County was 168; in Polk County, 137. In Gadsden County, where Gore picked up 153 net votes, officials had interpreted 187 total votes that had been rejected by the machines on Election Day, thus foreshadowing the manual recount controversies ahead. There were lesser Gore gains elsewhere, and in about two dozen counties—most of them rural—Bush had actually gained some votes.

Then came two disasters. Officials in Palm Beach County reported that their machine recount had provided a net gain of 859 votes for Gore, and those in Pinellas said that human error on election night had resulted in the failure to count several hundred absentee ballots that, when now run through the system, contributed to a net Gore recount gain of 478 votes.

Ginsberg, who had been trying frantically to keep abreast of developments in the counties, could not believe what he was seeing. Never in his experience had a lead the size of Bush's evaporated during what should have been a routine second run of the vote-tabulating equipment. Baker too could feel the whole thing slipping away. "They're stealing the election," he told Zoellick, not the last time he would express that sentiment and not the last time he would be wrong. As suddenly as it had started, the hemorrhaging stopped. In the final few counties to report, Bush actually picked up a handful of votes. The recount had devastated Bush's margin but not eliminated it. With all sixty-seven counties reporting, the Texas governor clung to a lead of just three hundred votes.

It had been a curious process. Three weeks after its end, the Bush Florida team would receive an unsolicited statistical analysis dated December 2, 2000, from a man identifying himself as Matthew Spiegel of the Yale School of Management. Himself a Democrat, Mr. Spiegel entitled his paper, "Are Chads Democrats? An Analysis of the Florida Presidential Recount." Reviewing the machine recount in every county, Spiegel concluded: "Estimates indicate that on average if a ballot's status changed from no vote to a vote, the chance that it went to Gore was about 15 percent higher than one would expect given his fraction of the county's vote. Overall then, controlling for each candidate's vote in a county and the type of ballot used, this paper estimates that Gore picked up 903 too many votes in the recount relative to what would have been expected by chance machine read errors."[7]

Viewed another way, Spiegel calculated that the recount had produced a total of 4,245 "revisions," defined as "any event that changes either candidate's total." Gore had picked up more than 1,400 votes in the recount, but according to Spiegel, "If the revisions are unbiased then the probability that 4,245 revisions events will produce 1,225 or more net positive outcomes for one candidate is about zero (t-statistic of 18.8). Even if you exclude both Palm Beach and Pinellas Counties on grounds that both are unusual for some reason there still remains almost no chance the results were due entirely to luck (*t*-statistic of 18.8)."[8] In layman's terms, the suggestion of wrongdoing was statistically persuasive.

But Spiegel's theory would never be tested. Although the Bush team took some perfunctory steps toward obtaining explanations from the two counties, they would for broader political reasons decide against demanding recounts in any of the sixty-seven counties. And since Palm Beach County was later subject to a complete manual recount, it is very likely that whatever glitch occurred during the electronic recount was rendered moot.

On November 9, even before the machine recount was completed, Gore raised the stakes. His team announced that it would ask for manual recounts in four counties: Volusia, Miami-Dade, Palm Beach, and Broward. Publicly, the Gore forces explained their choice of the four counties as though political calculations were the furthest thing from mind. "The only four counties in which hand counts were requested were counties where there was [*sic*] real anomalies that showed up—real irregularities,"[9] said Christopher on November 11. To reporters covering Gore's Florida challenge, however, the campaign made no effort to conceal the thinking behind its choice: These were the four counties where, considering both vote totals and percentages, Gore had made his strongest showings and where Democratic officials were in majority control of any recount process. A recount in each of the four counties, particularly one conducted under rules vesting considerable discretion in the counters, could generate hundreds, perhaps thousands, of additional votes for Gore, possibly providing him with a narrow victory.

In many ways Gore was following textbook political strategy. Small wonder. Three veteran Democratic trench warriors had written the booklet, *The Recount Primer*, in the mid-1990s: Timothy Downs, Chris Sautter, and John Hardin

Young. Hardin and Sautter were now members of the Gore Florida team. The booklet states "If a candidate is ahead, the scope of the recount should be as narrow as possible, and the rules and procedures of the recount should be the same as those used election night. A recount should duplicate the procedures of election night to correct arithmetical or counting errors."[10]

The trailing candidate takes the opposite approach: "If a candidate is behind, the scope should be as broad as possible, and the rules should be different from those used election night. A recount should be an audit of the election to ensure the accuracy and honesty of the results."[11]

Then why not seek recounts in all the counties rather than the four selected? "That's exactly what we should have done," Young later declared. "Sautter and I were screaming not to limit the recount." It has been speculated that Gore feared a public relations disaster should he seek to invoke recount procedures in all sixty-seven counties. And, of course, the decision whether or not to initiate the requested recounts would have rested with the individual canvassing boards, many controlled by Republicans. "I think Gore picked the places he thought might get him ahead quickly," recalled Young. "Once we're up for 24 hours, the entire dynamic of the fight changes."

For Baker, who suspected from the outset that the Gore Florida strategy amounted to little more than "slash and burn," the manual recount request confirmed those suspicions. More important, it laid to rest any notion of a three- or four-day confrontation after which the Bush team could go home a winner. This was becoming a war.

Wars need soldiers and officers, in this case lawyers, lawyers, and more lawyers. A good leadership cadre was already on hand or en route. Baker and Ginsberg, of course. Ted Cruz from the Bush campaign staff was also in Tallahassee. So were Bob Zoellick and George Terwilliger III, former Deputy Attorney General and now a senior partner with White and Case in Washington. Terwilliger's partner, Timothy Flanigan, was also on hand. Ted Olson, a tough trial and appellate lawyer from Washington, D.C., had been contacted while flying to Los Angeles and was now en route to Florida. Josh Bolten, of the Gore staff, would also soon arrive. One stroke of good luck was having Bobby Burchfield of Covington and Burling already in place in Miami. Burchfield, general counsel to President George Bush's 1992 reelection campaign, had spent election night in Austin preparing to celebrate the victory and was thus among the first of the lawyers to be sent to Florida. In Miami, he would join forces with Marcos Jimenez, a Miami-based White and Case partner, and Ken Mehlman, national field director of the Bush campaign, who would take charge of strategically deploying the Bush legal and political forces to wherever they were most needed in the state.

Now Baker and Ginsberg sent out an SOS for more lawyers—lawyers who would be ready to do battle for as long as it would take. Michael Carvin, a respected trial and appellate lawyer from Washington, was brought down. Soon Tallahassee was teeming with this "second wave" of lawyers, including John Bridgeland, Ken Juster, Alex Azar, Bill Kelley, John Bolton, Mike Madigan, and others. Some, like Bolton and Madigan, were sent to fight the ground wars in Palm Beach and Broward Counties; others—partners in some of the nation's most prestigious law firms—were asked to research legal issues, write briefs, compose "talking points," and generally perform the kind of work their own associates had been doing for them only days before. Baker next turned to his own law firm, Baker Botts, and brought in Kirk Van Thyne, who would play a critical role in coordinating legal research for the many court battles ahead. Eventually, Baker would bring from Houston and Chicago two teams of high-powered trial lawyers to handle the contest phase of the Gore challenge, demonstrating that his compartmentalized teams of specialists were more than a match for David Boies, who would become the "Jesus Christ Superstar" of the Gore team. "This was the biggest group of egos not flexing their egos I've ever been associated with," Ginsberg would later remark.

Within days, the Baker and Ginsberg recruits started pouring into Tallahassee, most winding up at the three-story red brick building that served as headquarters for the Republican Party in the lazy state capital. Office space was limited, secretarial help almost nonexistent, computers at a premium, and the mood of both the new arrivals and the veterans, surly and perplexed. "Tallahassee," noted John Bolton in his diary, "is a city where there are small armies of lawyers running around everywhere engaging in pitched battles with one another . . . and those are just the Republicans."

Enter Joe Allbaugh, Governor Bush's campaign manager. The crew-cut, husky former Marine began by "tossing everybody out," reassigning office space on the basis of priority, and locating enough office equipment to service a large law firm, which is exactly what the Tallahassee operation was becoming. Phone service was upgraded. Staffs of couriers and drivers appeared as if by magic. Secretaries came later. Most importantly, a three-meal-a-day catering service was initiated. There are today a score or so of Bush Florida veterans who can count on the fingers of one hand the number of restaurant meals they ate while in the state.

While the troops were assembling, Baker was now facing an urgent decision: how should the Bush team respond to the Gore demand for manual recounts? One option was to respond in kind, targeting a handful of Republican counties to offset whatever Gore might pick up in the Democratic strongholds. Baker intuitively disliked that option because it let Gore set the terms of the debate. "I thought we held the high moral ground," he would later recall. "Our position was: It's over. We won. Let's stop counting. Let's go home." His intuition was reinforced by advice from Cardenas, Enright, Jimenez, and other Republican strategists. The Republicans had been in overdrive working to get out the vote, they said. In nearly all precincts, they had exceeded their targets. They worried that there may be very few Republican votes left to be counted. Further, even in Republican counties, like Duval, a high percentage of the undervotes—those ballots containing no vote for the presidency—had been concentrated in Democratic precincts. Difficulty following voting instructions seemed to be correlated with language problems or illiteracy and the incidence of both was higher among Democrats.

The Bush team would not demand any manual recounts. That meant a redoubled effort to block Gore from having his selected counties conduct their own. Here Baker saw as key allies Katherine Harris, the Secretary of State, and L. Clayton Roberts, Director of the Division of Elections. Harris had served as one of Bush's eight state cochairmen, a Florida political tradition which nonetheless would provide ammunition for charges of bias by Gore and his allies, part of an ugly campaign of character assassination waged by high-ranking Democrats and even many in the press whose own impartiality is, at the very least, open to question.

The question of enforcement of the seven-day statutory deadline for completing recounts would come to dominate the legal battle through the end of the protest period. The initial determination involved the circumstances under which a full county recount could be undertaken. There was little doubt that under Florida law the county canvassing boards had absolute discretion to decline to begin a recount.[12] Once they decided to honor the request, they were obligated to manually recount at least three precincts designated by the protesting candidate amounting to at least one percent of the county vote. Florida law provides "that if the manual recount indicates an error in the vote tabulation which could affect the outcome of the election, the county canvassing board shall: (a) correct the error and recount the remaining precincts with the vote tabulation system; (b) request the Department of State to verify the tabulation software; or (c) manually recount all ballots."[13] The critical early question was whether "error in vote tabulation" meant only a problem where the vote tabulation equipment failed to count a properly marked ballot or whether it included the failure to count ballots where the voter had failed to follow instructions but where visual inspection of the ballot could indicate the voter's intent to vote for one candidate. Shaping up, Baker and his fellow lawyers concluded, was a potential fight between the Secretary of State and the Gore lawyers, which called for no immediate Bush action at the state level.

That left the question as to whether Bush should initiate action in the federal courts seeking to block the manual re-counts. The team on hand quickly found itself divided. Zoellick, Flanigan, and Josh Bolten had difficulty finding a federal question. After all, there were dozens of states with recount provisions, most involving manual recounts, and Florida's was just beginning in Volusia and Palm Beach counties, the two counties that had decided to proceed. At the very least, resorting to the federal courts was prema-ture, because Bush had as yet suffered no demonstrable harm. An early loss in the federal courts could set the tone for a consideration of election issues by a far less sympa-thetic state Supreme Court. Indeed, the latter court could regard such a federal decision as precedent for a decision against Bush. Moreover, advocates of the federal gambit were undermining conservative legal theory endorsed by Bush, which frowns on federal preemption of state issues and prerogatives.

Another experienced appellate lawyer, Mike Carvin, also thought the federal case was weak. There is no way to plau-sibly argue that manual recounts are unconstitutional, he maintained. Four-fifths of the country uses them. The only argument against manual recounts is that the standards dif-fer from place to place depending on who is doing the count-ing. And that's a long shot.

Further, there was a chance that a challenge to existing Florida law would backfire. One of the principal Bush assets in the state was the Republican-dominated state legislature. And here were the Bush forces about to target as unconsti-tutional a statute enacted by that legislature. Would that un-dermine the legislature's authority? Would it encourage the Florida Supreme Court to tamper with state legislation in order to correct some deficiency depicted by Bush's own lawyers? The move to invoke federal power was not merely a long shot; it was a serious potential risk, which should not be lightly taken.

Baker, Terwilliger, and Olson came down on the other side. From the outset, Terwilliger felt that the case would wind up in the federal courts and it might just as well be on a series of legal issues framed by the Bush forces. Olson had confidence in the brain trust's ability to come up with a federal issue, though at the outset he couldn't identify one with much precision.

Baker's view was more pragmatic. He thought this was the moment to expand the Bush options, not to foreclose even one. The Florida battle could be resolved by actions of the Secretary of State or the Florida legislature. It could be resolved by one of the candidates faced with public impatience with his fight, or even the impatience of his own party. It could come down to a decision of the Florida Supreme Court or the Supreme Court of the United States. Of these possibilities, the state Supreme Court seemed the least promising to Baker. He had already been told about its penchant for liberal activism. What's more, Baker had once been a close friend with Florida's late Governor Lawton Chiles. The two had regularly attended prayer breakfasts in Washington during Chiles's senatorial years (another regular participant had been Senator Al Gore). Baker had also found in Chiles an enthusiastic fellow turkey hunter and on at least one Florida shoot, Chiles had brought along his friend and counsel, W. Dexter Douglas. "Dexter is a liberal southern Democrat," Baker later recalled, "and I knew he had recommended to Lawton six of the seven justices now on the Florida Supreme Court. So I was wary of that group."

Baker called Bush on the night of November 9 to bring him up to date on the debate. Bush deferred to the legal and political advice of his family friend. If Baker was saying go to the federal courts, that was good enough for the Governor of Texas.

Baker's final objective in connection with the federal lawsuit was to bring in an outside lawyer of great stature to argue the case alongside Olson, "a Charles Allen Wright" type as he later would say. Wright, the late, great Texas legal scholar, had represented Richard Nixon in two historic cases, the Pentagon Papers and the Watergate Tapes disputes, majestically losing both. Baker settled on former Senator John Danforth, a well-liked and fair-minded man, but hardly a constitutional giant. Baker found Danforth vacationing in Cancun and asked him whether he would consider flying to Florida to help represent Bush. Danforth instead began lecturing Baker on the folly of the case and how it would backfire politically and hurt Bush, preventing this young man who had run so credible a campaign from ever again seeking the nation's highest office. Baker decided that Danforth and Cancun deserved each other and made no further effort to interrupt the Missourian's vacation. The ball was then in Olson's hands. Olson set off for Miami to file his motion in the U.S. District Court for the Southern District of Florida. Baker asked his staff to prepare a statement for the press announcing the decision to go to court. At the GOP headquarters in Tallahassee and in law offices there and in Miami and Washington, computers ran all night and lawyers, who might be charging private clients $500 per hour for similar services, pecked away at their keyboards.

The following day, Olson strode into court with a thick legal packet including his motion, such legal precedent as could be assembled to support it, and a number of affidavits documenting the chaos that the Bush team claimed was resulting from reliance on manual recounts. With additions and variations, this would be the kind of material he would bring to the United States Supreme Court the following month when the presidency would hang in the balance.

CHAPTER 2

Defining the Issues

The results of the recount reported on November 10 showed Bush with a lead of three hundred votes. With the final crop of military-dominated absentee ballots not scheduled for counting until ten days after the election, Bush's only fear was a series of tricky and dilatory Gore moves that could endanger if not overturn the results. So as Olson finished preparations to launch his federal suit to be filed Saturday, November 11, Bush and Baker moved in concert to redefine the political landscape on which the post-election battle was being fought. They sought to mobilize public opinion. No longer would Gore's challenges be indulged as a reasonable test of the accuracy of Tuesday's count. Now they would be characterized as an act of self-indulgence, a willingness to exploit every loophole in the law to produce a result that reflected what Gore wished had happened on Tuesday instead of what did happen. In fact, as the absentee ballots would confirm, George W. Bush was the winner. It was time to move on to the transition period so the new president could begin putting together his administration. The cost of delay would be a prolonged period of instability, which would be damaging to the nation at home and abroad.

"The vote here in Florida was very close, but when it was counted, Governor Bush was the winner," Baker declared on November 10. "For the good of the country and for the sake of our standing in the world, the campaigning should end and the business of an orderly transition should begin." Baker urged the country to "step back for a minute and pause and think about what's at stake here. . . . The purpose of our national election is to establish a constitutional government, not unending legal wrangling." Baker acknowledged that the Bush team was contemplating a resort to the federal courts challenging manual recounts. "The more often ballots are recounted, especially by hand, the more likely it is that human errors, like lost ballots and other risks, will be introduced. This frustrates the very reason why we have moved from hand counting to machine counting."[1]

In Austin, Bush brought his chief of staff, Andrew Card, top economic advisor Lawrence Lindsey, national security advisor Condoleezza Rice, domestic advisor Clay Johnson, and his running mate Dick Cheney before reporters as a way of underlining the message that the race was over and that the transition to the Bush administration had begun. "There was a count on election night and there's been a recount in Florida and I understand there are still votes to be counted, but I'm in the process of planning, in a responsible way, a potential administration," Bush said. "And I think that's what the country needs to know, that this administration will be ready to assume office and be prepared to lead." Bush did stop short of urging Gore to fold his tent. "You know, I think each candidate and each team is going to have to do what they think is best—in the best interests of the country,"[2] he said. But neither Baker nor Cheney had similar inhibitions; like tag-team wrestlers, they would take turns during the weeks ahead urging Gore to end his challenge to the Florida vote.

Bush's "let's move on" message would wax and wane over the next month in synchronization with the ebb and flow of the legal and political tide in Florida. As a counter to the Gore "count every vote" mantra, it worked reasonably well.

Polls would show a modest but steady majority supporting the notion that the legal wrangling should end and that Bush should be declared the winner in Florida and in the presidential contest. And while Gore through supreme personal effort was able to sustain support for his Florida contest from his own party leaders and the editorial boards of newspapers that had supported his candidacy, there was a time-urgent quality to his effort that may have led his legal team to impose unnecessarily harsh deadlines on their claims for relief—deadlines later adopted by both state and federal courts.

By the time Olson filed his suit November 11, recounts were underway in Volusia and Palm Beach counties, and Broward and Miami-Dade had not yet decided whether to undertake full manual recounts. Baker sought to put the best light on what he knew would be accusations from the Gore camp that he was seeking to block a fair vote count. "The manual vote count sought by the Gore campaign would not be more accurate than an automated count," Baker told reporters. "Indeed it would be less fair and less accurate. Human error, individual subjectivity, and decisions to 'determine the voter's intent' would replace precision machinery in tabulating millions of small marks and fragile hole punches."[3]

The Gore camp was quick to strike back, with Daley and Christopher convening a press conference. "If Governor Bush truly believes he has won the election in Florida, he should not have any reason to doubt or to fear to have the machine count checked by a hand count," said Christopher. "This procedure is authorized under Florida law, under Texas law, and under the law of many other jurisdictions."[4]

The Texas statute, passed during the administration of Governor George W. Bush, was something of an embarrassment despite Baker's reply that, unlike Florida, the Texas law "sets out some objective standards to guide the election officials in performing the recount. It doesn't just give them carte blanche authority, so that they can come in, and through human error or even, indeed, mischief, count ballots for whomever they favor."[5]

In fact, the Texas law simply forbids the categorical exclusion of dimpled chads, permitting their inclusion when there is independent evidence of voter intent.

Bush and Cheney and Republican voters in the four counties selected by Gore were the principal plaintiffs in the Olson complaint. They claimed that the manual recounts provided so much latitude to the counters as to violate the Due Process and Equal Protection clauses of the Fourteenth Amendment. They further claimed that by undermining the right to vote, the recount was interfering with the right to assemble peaceably guaranteed by the First Amendment, a Christmas tree legal ornament if ever one existed. Bush voters from other counties also joined the suit as plaintiffs, claiming that by generating additional votes for Gore in the selected counties, the manual recounts would dilute the value of their own ballots. This was the legal theory behind many of the successful "one man, one vote" decisions of the 1960s. This Equal Protection argument would remain pertinent for the remainder of the litigation.

The abuses alleged in the Olson pleadings were largely theoretical, because the counting was only beginning in three of the counties on the date his motion was filed before District Court Judge Donald M. Middlebrooks, a Clinton appointee. But by oral argument time counsel could draw on a few real examples. These included the apparent mutilation of ballots in the process of being counted, the failure to keep orderly records of objections by Bush observers, and most important, the nearly standardless discretion afforded members of the three-person canvassing commissions to determine which ballots should be counted and which should not.

Drawing on affidavits from his observers in the field as well as statements by officials themselves, Olson documented a change in the method of counting Palm Beach County ballots from the guidelines that had governed counting there since 1990. The question involved marks made on a section of the voting card known as a "chad," a word that would quickly ingratiate itself into the lexicon of American politics as well as late-night television comedy. In counties using voting cards that had to be punched through with the aid of a blunt-edged instrument called a stylus, voters were instructed to punch the stylus down through the card next to the preferred candidate or issue position they supported. Problems could arise when the area behind the hole—the chad—was not completely punched through or dislodged, in some cases exhibiting no more than a small indentation or dimple. But voters who started to punch their ballots for a candidate and then changed their minds, or some who carelessly scratched an area near one hole or another could also leave dimpled chads. In her *Guidelines on Ballots with Chads Not Completely Removed,* written November 2, 1990, Theresa LePore, the Palm Beach County Supervisor of Elections, wrote

> The guidelines assume that these directions have been understood and followed. Therefore, a chad that is hanging or partially punched **may** be counted as a vote, since it is possible to punch through the card and still not totally dislodge the chad. But a chad that is fully attached, bearing only an indentation, should not be counted as a vote. An indentation may result from a voter placing the stylus in the position, but not punching through. Thus an indentation is not evidence of intent to cast a valid vote.

Now, a decade later, Palm Beach County was considering a more lax standard while the other counties wrestled with the question of what standards to use. In the end, Palm Beach would change the old LePore standard only slightly, deciding—in most but not all cases—to count dimpled chads when a pattern of such indentations suggested the voter thought a light brush with the stylus was sufficient to vote. Broward, on the other hand, would count dimpled chads, or even marks near a perforation, as valid votes if they appeared to conform to the political profile of the remainder of the ballot.

The question of change would prove significant because federal law stipulated that the Congress would confer conclusively presumptive legitimacy (a "safe harbor") for any state electors chosen under rules in place prior to the November vote.[6] Whether Florida had defied that principle either through its manual recount rules or by the Florida Supreme Court extending the deadline for such recounts to be completed became important issues in subsequent litigation before the U.S. Supreme Court.

Hardly had the oral arguments before him been completed than Judge Middlebrooks, in a twenty-four-page opinion, denied the Bush injunction request. Relying largely on points made in the brief filed on behalf of Vice President Gore, the court first noted the extremely high burden on the part of one seeking to enjoin a recount to show his constitutional argument will prevail and the greatly proscribed role of the federal courts in tampering with state election practices. As to the heart of the Olson argument, "that Florida's decentralized county-by-county electoral system can yield disparate tabulating results from county to county," and that the counting of previously discarded ballots in one selected county but not another, dilutes the vote of the latter, the court said that was a reasonable price to pay for decentralization. After all, said the court, both the Constitution and the Congress have made the individual states supreme in this area:

> Unless and until each electoral county in the United States uses the exact same automatic tabulation (and even then there may be system malfunctions and the like), there will be tabulating discrepancies depending on the method of tabulation. Rather than a sign of weakness or constitutional injury, some solace can be taken in the fact that no one centralized body or person can control the tabulation of an entire statewide or national election. For the more county boards and individuals involved in the electoral regulation process, the less likely it becomes that corruption, bias, or error can influence the ultimate result of the election.[7]

Judge Middlebrooks denied the relief sought and Olson began an appeal to the Atlanta-based U.S. Court of Appeals for the Eleventh Circuit. Neither he nor Baker and Ginsberg were particularly surprised by the outcome, but Judge Middlebrook's decision had come closer to adjudicating the merits of the case than they would have wished.

While the Bush team was assuring itself access to the federal courts, both sides began jockeying for position on two issues central to whether Gore would get the recounts he sought during the so-called protest phase of the post-election period. The first was whether the ability to discern a voter's preference in the presidential contest after the machines had discarded the ballot as an undervote exposed the sort of "error in vote tabulation" that could justify a manual recount. The second was the extent to which the Secretary of State was compelled to exercise her discretion to include the results of manual recounts not completed within the statutory period of seven days from the election.

Both questions placed Secretary of State Katherine Harris in the eye of the political storm and in the cross hairs of the big Democratic guns. Before the Florida Courts appropriated her issues, Harris would find herself called a "hack" and a "lackey for George W. Bush" by Gore's press spokesman, Chris Lehane, who also likened her to a "Soviet commissar." The liberal press seemed endlessly fascinated by her eyebrows, her makeup, her pumps, and her dresses. Former Clinton aide Paul Begala said she looked like "Cruella De Vil coming to steal the puppies." Harvard law professor Alan Dershowitz called her "a crook."[8]

Ms. Harris had, in part, brought the problem upon herself, not only by having served as one of Bush's eight cochairmen in the state, but also by having campaigned for him in New Hampshire. But she was no cipher. Far more independent and strong-willed than given credit for, Harris had defied Jeb Bush to defeat his candidate for the Secretary of State's job, a perch from which she hoped to vault to a position as an international trade negotiator in a Republican administration. It was at a Republican Institute session on trade where she met Robert Zoellick, who regarded her as intelligent and strong-willed, but sometimes lacking in self-confidence. He, Allbaugh, and Baker paid a courtesy call on her in Florida, where he recalls telling Harris, "You are going to be under incredible pressure. Get the best legal help you can, take your position, and stick to it. Once you start moving, you'll never get your feet back on the ground."

Harris took Zoellick's advice to heart and retained Joe Klock of Miami, a slightly rumpled, plain-spoken, passionate Democrat whose knowledge of state election law is encyclopedic. Klock told Harris to avoid all further contact with the Bush team and assured her that he would not allow her to issue any ruling or opinion inconsistent with Florida statutory and case law, as he and his partners and associates understood it.

Harris and L. Clayton Roberts, the director of the Division of Elections, dealt first with the question of whether the term "error in voting tabulation" justifying a manual recount included situations where the failure to count the vote was due to voter error in punching the ballot. The issue had been raised in letters from Al Cardenas, the GOP State Chairman, and Judge Charles E. Burton, Chairperson of the Palm Beach County Canvassing Board, requesting advisory opinions. As would also be the case in Broward and Miami-Dade Counties, the four-precinct Palm Beach County sample had found no problems with tabulation hardware or software, only some number of improperly punched ballots where voter intent could still be determined.

With Harris's approval and on the basis of Klock's legal analysis, Roberts replied to Cardenas on November 13, "An 'error in the vote tabulation' means a counting error in which the vote tabulation equipment fails to count properly marked marksense or properly punched punchcard ballots. . . . The inability of voting systems to read improperly marked marksense or improperly punched punchcard ballot is not a 'error in vote tabulation.' . . ."[9] Thus, a ballot adorned with pregnant or dimpled chads rather than properly punched holes could not trigger the full recount provided for by statute. Similar letters were sent to Burton and Jane Carroll, the supervisor of elections for Broward county. Klock's reasoning was that the statute had been amended after the 1988 McKay-Mack contest to provide a recount remedy for instances where the vote tabulation equipment is found to be defective, as had been the case in that election. Further, the companion remedies, authorizing the canvassing boards to "correct the error and recount the remaining precincts with the vote tabulation system," or to "request the Department of State to verify the tabulation software," were clearly directed at errors in the equipment.

The Harris-Roberts view, had it prevailed, could well have resolved the Florida battle on the spot, but it was immediately challenged by an opinion from Attorney General Robert A. Butterworth, who had been state chairman of the Gore campaign. Strangely, no one termed Butterworth a "hack," a "commissar," or a "crook," no one seemed to care a whit about the way he dressed, and no one suggested that he was being manipulated like a puppet by his political masters. Indeed, only a few intrepid souls thought it noteworthy that Butterworth's entrance into the manual recount debate was highly officious, because such matters were totally beyond his jurisdiction, his own Web site advising that "questions under the Florida Election Code should be directed to the Division of Elections in the Department of State." Also responding to a letter from Judge Burton, Butterworth, on November 14, concluded that the Division of Elections interpretation was "clearly at variance with Florida statutes and case law," and insisted that the term "error in vote tabulation" includes "a discrepancy between the number of votes determined by a vote tabulation system and the number of votes determined by a manual count of a sampling of precincts."[10]

Virtually ignored at the time was a second letter sent by Butterworth to Judge Burton outlining the legal dangers ahead should Florida proceed with its system of manual recounts in a handful of counties, or what Butterworth termed a "two-tier system." He wrote:

> A two-tier system would have the effect of treating voters differently, depending upon what county they voted in. A voter in a county where a manual count was conducted would benefit from

having a better chance of having his or her vote actually counted than a voter in a county where a hand count was halted.

As the State's chief legal officer, I feel a duty to warn that if the final certified total for balloting in the State of Florida includes figures generated from this two-tier system of differing behavior by official canvassing boards, the State will incur a legal jeopardy, under both the U.S. and State constitutions. This legal jeopardy could potentially lead to Florida having all of its votes, in effect, disqualified and this state being barred from the Electoral College's selection of a President.[11]

While Butterworth was specifically addressing a situation where one county granted a request for a manual recount and another didn't, his legal logic ran parallel to that of Bush and his team. It was to be analysis later shared by both the Florida and U. S. Supreme Courts. Either Gore and his legal team deluded themselves into thinking they could get by gaming the system as one would a race for county sheriff, or they were convinced that if they could quickly capture the lead, Bush would never be able to dislodge them.

The Harris and Butterworth opinions on the definition of "error in vote tabulation" came only a day apart. With no additional delay, Palm Beach County took the precaution of obtaining an order from Circuit Court Judge Jorge Labarga permitting the count to begin. The second matter involving the Secretary's discretion whether or not to wave statutory deadlines for the certification of manual recounts would become one of the defining issues in the battle. Florida law unambiguously requires each county to file its returns with the secretary of state as soon as they are counted. Each canvassing board then has a week to officially certify the returns, which must be filed with the secretary of state. But what if a county misses the deadline? Under one provision of the Florida Code, "If the county returns are not received by the Department of State by 5 P.M. of the seventh day following an election, all missing counties **shall** be ignored (emphasis added), and the results shown by the returns on file shall be certified." But another provision, passed several years later, states that when a county misses the seven-day 5 P.M. deadline, "such returns **may** be ignored (emphasis added) and the results on file at that time may be certified by the department."[12]

The Gore people and officials in at least three of the counties selected for manual recounts quickly realized that strict adherence to the seven-day deadline would doom their effort. While Gore had requested the recounts within the prescribed seventy-two-hour window, only Volusia had moved promptly to take the sample precinct counts and begin the larger effort. The other three counties would have had great difficulty establishing they had made a good faith effort to meet the deadline had anyone demanded such a showing. Palm Beach County had decided on November 9 to conduct the partial recount necessary to establish a predicate for the full recount but delayed five days before starting the real thing. Broward County commenced its full recount on November 15, missing the statutory deadline by a full day, after first voting not to proceed because the sample count had turned up only four net additional votes for Gore. The Miami-Dade County Canvassing Board held its decision meeting on November 14, the day of the statutory deadline, and decided not to proceed with the manual recount. Three days later, after considerable pressure from the Gore camp and political demonstrations throughout the area, the board reversed its decision.

Harris met with both camps on November 13, informing them that she intended to stick to the November 14 deadline. Publicly, the Gore camp reacted angrily. "Her plan, I'm afraid, has the look of an effort to produce a particular result in the election," said Daley, "rather than to ensure that the voice of all the citizens of the state would be heard." Daley charged Harris with "another effort in a series of efforts to obstruct the work of these counties to count the votes of the people of Florida."[13] He said the Gore people would likely challenge Harris's decision in the Florida courts.

Meanwhile, members of the Bush legal team were dismayed that Harris was telegraphing her punches, giving both the Gore people and the Florida judiciary time to contemplate their next move. "We might have been better off if the secretary of state had simply allowed the counting to go on and then certified the results when the statutory deadline occurred without the manual recounts having been completed," said Ken Juster, who was involved in marshalling arguments that went into the Bush court battles.

Baker and his team also took note as Gore brought in David Boies, a heavyweight trial and appellate lawyer from New York, to assume the role of legal quarterback. Fresh from a massive federal district court victory in the Microsoft antitrust case, Boies would combine courtroom skill with an affinity for spinning the press. Baker made a mental note to find lawyers familiar with Boies's technique. He found one, Irv Terrell, in his own firm and another, Phil Beck, a distinguished Chicago trial lawyer. Both had notches in their belt with the Boies name on it. Without fanfare or a great deal of Larry King-type hullabaloo, Baker would bring both to Tallahassee, where each would continue his winning streak against Boies.

Circuit Court Judge Terry Lewis, a respected jurist and middle-of-the-road Democrat, was given jurisdiction of the Gore motion for a preliminary injunction blocking Harris from certifying the Florida results until the manual recounts were tabulated. Harris took something of an absolutist view of her discretion under Florida law, claiming that absent an act of God, she could extend the deadline for manual recounts or decline to do so as she saw fit. This was further than Lewis was willing to go. On November 14, he issued an order requiring the canvassing boards to file their incomplete returns that evening, but to keep counting past the deadline and to submit amended returns when their recount was completed. "The secretary of state may ignore such late-filed returns, but may not do so arbitrarily, rather only by the proper exercise of her discretion after consideration of all appropriate facts and circumstances."[14]

Now Lewis introduced a theme that the Gore team would emphasize when the case reached the state Supreme Court and which that Court would seize as its own. A candidate had three days under Florida law to request a recount. Full consideration of that request could delay commencement of the recount until the very eve of the deadline, functionally eliminating the more populous counties from completing it on time. "It is unlikely that the legislature would give the right to protest returns, but make it meaningless because it could not be acted upon in time," wrote Lewis. "To determine ahead of time that such returns will be ignored, however, unless caused by some act of God, is not the exercise of discretion. It is the abdication of that discretion." He further warned Harris that the Florida Supreme Court has held that "substantial compliance" is sufficient to comply with a mandatory filing deadline.

Lewis then presented Harris with a virtual blueprint for winning her case in his court and insulating herself against state Supreme Court reversal. He did so by suggesting a series of questions she might address in exercising her discretion: "If the returns are received from a county at 5:05 P.M. on November 14, 2000, should the results be ignored? What about fifteen minutes? An hour? What if there was an electrical power outage? Some other malfunction of the transmitting equipment? More particularly related to this case, when was the request for recount made? What were the reasons given? When did the Canvassing Board decide to do a manual recount? What was the basis for determination that such a recount was the appropriate action? How late were the results?"[15] Had Harris addressed each of these questions in specific terms rather than rejecting categorically the idea of extending the deadline in anything less than cataclysmic circumstances, she would have fortified Lewis' subsequent decision in her favor, making it tougher even for an activist Florida Supreme Court to credibly reverse the Circuit Court.

Even the state that hosts the Grapefruit League had rarely seen so many fat pitches served up in a single appearance at the plate. Harris could well have kept silent, allowing the process to continue for a few days while awaiting the final batch of absentee ballots. Palm Beach, Broward, and Miami-Dade counties would by then have been three days past the original deadline with no end imminent and with no real excuses for the substantial delay. Miami-Dade and Broward had first voted to reject the manual recounts. Indeed, Broward had reversed itself after the sample precincts had failed to meet the statutory criterion for initiating the full manual recount. And Palm Beach had sleepwalked its way past the deadlines, not even beginning its recount until the critical moment was at hand. Again, had Harris chosen that route, it is difficult to see how even an activist state Supreme Court could have found any abuse of discretion.

Instead, Klock decided to substitute precedent for the sort of freewheeling discretion Lewis had urged. By 5:00 P.M. that evening, Volusia County had completed its recount, meeting the statutory deadline and providing Gore with an additional 98 votes. Harris then announced that her director of elections had instructed the three remaining counties to state their reasons in writing for failing to meet the deadline and to have the documents in her hand by 2:00 P.M. November 15.

> Unless I determine in the exercise of my discretion that these facts and circumstances contained within these written statements justify an amendment to today's official returns, the State Elections Canvassing Commission, in a manner consistent with its usual and normal practice, will certify statewide returns reported to this office today. Subsequently, the overseas ballots that are due by midnight Friday will also be certified and the final results of the election for President of the United States of America in the state of Florida will be announced.[16]

Harris's purpose in devising this two-stage certification was clear: had she waited until the absentee ballots were counted, she might well have received completed manual recounts and then decided they were too late to be counted, which would have put her in a politically and—most likely—legally untenable position.

Almost as a footnote to her day's activities, Harris filed a motion with the Florida Supreme Court asking it to block the continuing manual recounts, or barring that, to mandate a single statewide standard for counting undervotes, and to consolidate all the election cases in Tallahassee's Leon County. The Court rejected her motion the following day.

The Gore camp, which of course wanted Harris to simply accept the late recounts, complained about her request for letters from the counties about to miss the deadline. Daley called her action "unfortunate and inexplicable." The Bush camp was no less upset. Already concerned about Harris telegraphing her punches, they shuddered to think that she had tried to consolidate and expedite all the legal activity in Florida. Their strategy was to let the clock wind down, not to find new ways to grease the mechanism. Moreover, Judge Lewis' ruling posed some danger. Not only had he let the re-counts continue past the deadline, he seemed to want Harris to exercise her discretion broadly and forgivingly, coming down on the side of counting votes rather than on the side they preferred—of finality of process.

Harris received letters of explanation from the three counties still recounting and promptly announced that they were "insufficient to warrant the waiver of the unambiguous filing deadline."[17] Klock had thoroughly researched Florida case law to determine the grounds on which extensions had been approved in the past. Those cases involved proof of voter fraud that might have affected the election's outcome, indications of substantial noncompliance with election procedures that cast doubt on whether the election expressed the will of the voters, or situations involving circumstances beyond the control of election officials, such as an act of God, a power failure, or an equipment or mechanical malfunction that interfered with the good faith efforts of officials to complete the recount on time.

In tailoring the Harris response to a narrow reading of Florida precedent, Klock had given both Lewis and potentially the Florida Supreme Court some elbow room to overturn her ruling. He had also given the Bush team, as parties to the dispute, the task of defending a ruling the Bush lawyers might have written differently. Klock had drawn his legal authority from cases involving election *contests* in the courts where overturning an election result requires clear proof that the will of the electorate was thwarted. Thus Harris had ignored most of the recommended questions Judge Lewis had laid out for her. Even more to the point, many Bush lawyers concluded that there was no compelling reason for her to say anything. Their advice to Harris would have been to just sit tight, count the absentee ballots on Friday, certify the election, and get out of Dodge. "Reporters tended to assume a degree of coordination between ourselves and the secretary of state that simply didn't exist," a Bush lawyer later confided. "To a lesser extent, that was true of the state legislature too. We certainly were in contact. But while our interests overlapped, they were not identical."

The Florida sparring was punctuated by a moment of political drama on November 15 as Gore strode before television cameras at the White House shortly after the 6:30 P.M. network newscasts hit the air, and offered to end the legal battles in Florida if Bush would accept the recount results from Palm Beach, Broward, and Miami-Dade counties, or agree to a statewide manual recount. "We need a resolution that is fair and final," said Gore. "We need to move expeditiously to the most complete and accurate count that is possible."[18] Gore also proposed a private meeting with Bush.

Both in Tallahassee and in Waco, Texas, where Bush had been working from his ranch, Gore's proposals were viewed as a political stunt, not unlike Baker's "generous" offer earlier in the week to accept manual recounts completed by the November 14 deadline if Gore would agree to quit pressing for recounts anywhere else. Were he serious, he would have first contacted Bush to explore whether agreement in principle was possible and whether any accord on modalities—including counting rules—could be achieved. Now Gore wanted Bush to give up his legal and constitutional claims and drop his federal suit for the privilege of giving Gore precisely what he was seeking in the first place and with no accord on standards. Moreover, the 72-hour deadline for requesting manual recounts had long since passed, so Gore was cavalierly suggesting a remedy illegal under Florida law. And even if the parties should wait to the post-certification contest phase before seeking statewide manual recounts, at that stage only the candidate who lost the certification battle had the right to request anything. So the offer that gave Gore's supporters some rhetorical ammunition was as close to a facetious proposal as one could imagine.

Yet Bush had to reply publicly, so as aides worked preparing his remarks, Bush sped the nearly one hundred miles to the governor's mansion to deliver his prime-time reply live. Noting that he had prevailed not only on election day, but following multiple recounts in some counties, Bush said the good of the country required "a point of conclusion, a moment when America and the world know who is the next president." He continued: "I was encouraged tonight that Vice President Gore called for a conclusion to this process. We all agree. Unfortunately, what the Vice President proposed is exactly what he's been proposing all along: continuing with selective hand recounts that that are neither fair nor accurate, or compounding the error by extending a flawed process statewide."[19]

The consensus at the Tallahassee headquarters was that Bush had come out of the evening fairly well, given that the advantage usually rests with the attacker. The common assessment was that he had appeared a bit nervous; like a deer in the headlights. But Gore had nothing to show for his night's work except, perhaps, a consensus from restless Democrats to fight on. Bush faced no similar problem with party cohesion. Also, the Governor had again spelled out what was at heart a fairly difficult case to sell. Selective recounts are problematic because they discriminate against voters in counties that rely exclusively on the machine tallies. But extending the recount to every county is worse because the process itself is hopelessly flawed. It was a political sell that

Bush seemed able to make effectively to the constituencies he most cared about. But how would it play in the courts?

David Boies now led his team into action against Katherine Harris, claiming that she had failed to obey Judge Lewis's order to exercise her discretion as to whether or not to count late-filed recount results, instead treating the issue with a closed mind. He filed with Judge Lewis an emergency motion to compel compliance with his injunction. Stunningly, the Gore counsel also urged that Harris be held in contempt. Lewis said he would issue his opinion at 10:00 A.M. on November 17.

While both sides awaited Lewis's decision, the Florida Supreme Court on November 16 issued a unanimous, one-paragraph ruling permitting the recounts in Palm Beach and Broward Counties to continue. The Gore camp, beginning to sense a trend in state court rulings, thought Friday would bring a favorable decision from the circuit court.

But Lewis gave short shrift to the Gore case. Noting the "broad discretionary authority" vested in the secretary of state, Lewis held: "On the limited evidence presented, it appears that the Secretary has exercised her reasoned judgment to determine what relevant factors and criteria should be considered, applied them to the facts and circumstances pertinent to the individual counties involved, and made her decision. My order requires nothing more."[20] The Boies motion was rejected.

The GOP headquarters exploded with joy. War whoops were shouted and high fives exchanged. The press was reporting that Boies planned no immediate appeal to the state Supreme Court. The reason, most at Bush headquarters felt, was that he knew he had no case. Now Harris could finish tallying the absentee ballots, where Bush was expected to pick up between 500 and 1,000 votes, and certify the governor as the winner. Did that mean it was all over, or would be in another 24 hours? Not quite. There was still a contest period ahead, and who knew what Gore and his trial lawyers had up their sleeves. Nonetheless, the victory was one hell of a momentum builder.

The euphoria was short-lived. At 4:00 P.M. the Florida Supreme Court, without being asked, issued the following Stay Order: "In order to maintain the status quo, the Court, on its own motion, enjoins the Respondent, Secretary of State and Respondent, the Elections Canvassing Commission, from certifying the results of the November 7, 2000 presidential election, until further order of this Court. It is NOT the intent of this Order to stop the counting and conveying to the Secretary of State the results of absentee ballots or any other ballots."

Baker delivered a mandatory public statement putting what had been a hefty blow to the solar plexus in the best light. He suggested that "the court's action is designed to maintain the status quo until its hearing on Monday." Although neither side had requested the order, the action "is not an order on the merits of the case. We remain confident that, for all of the reasons discussed by the trial court in its two opinions, the Supreme Court will find that the secretary of state properly exercised her discretion and followed the law."

In fact, however, the Florida Supreme Court order left no grounds for self-deception among members of the Bush team. Instead of certification and a big step toward victory, the weekend would be spent writing briefs and keeping an eye on the recount proceedings now under way in all three counties. Further, it was the sort of order, undertaken with no request from the Gore team, that provided a revealing glimpse as to how the Court was likely to rule on the merits.

The briefs were due Sunday with oral argument scheduled for Monday. Mike Carvin would present most of the Bush case, with Richard adding a few words and Klock representing Harris. The sua sponte stay order of the Court had done little to shake Carvin's confidence. "I've done a lot of redistricting, which is very political, and a lot of civil rights, which is very ideological, but this was the simplest case of statutory construction I've ever seen," he recalled. "To lose this case, you'd have to have an utterly lawless court." As more colleagues who knew the court portrayed it as seven activists running out of control, Carvin began to develop doubts. Richard tried to reassure him, saying the Court was liberal but not partisan. His doubts intensified on the day of the oral argument when a colleague handed him a note saying the decision had already been written: it was 7–0 for Gore with a five-day deadline for completing the count.

In truth, Baker had been so convinced that the "Florida Supremes"—a term of non-endearment invariably used by the Bush team in private conversation—would rule for Gore that he had instructed aides to draft a statement blasting the Court for use after its decision came down. He also became more convinced that the U.S. Supreme Court would ultimately resolve the case and instructed Carvin to make certain he preserved the potential federal points in his oral argument. Both Baker and his colleagues still maintained a long-shot hope for the best, but they were already looking past the Florida Supreme Court to the nine-member U.S. Supreme Court in Washington.

CHAPTER 3

Rewriting the Law

It has long been a humorous adage among lawyers that when the law is against you, argue the facts, when the facts are against you, argue the law, and when both are against you, pound the table. A reading of the Gore/Boies brief and a review of Boies's oral argument before the Florida Supreme Court suggests a bit of tinkering with the third prong: when both the law and the facts are against you, argue that some guiding value transcends the importance of both. Thus did Boies contend that the right to vote and to have one's vote counted is more important than a "hypertechnical compliance" with a deadline in the law. Despite clear statutory language to the contrary, the brief argued that "the secretary has no discretion to reject the results of a manual recount." Otherwise the law would permit the secretary "to reject ballots that are conceded to have been validly cast, and that were identified in a properly initiated and conducted recount, simply because they reached the secretary later than a deadline so short as to preclude the completion of the recounts provided for by statute."[1]

The Boies brief further argued, with no ascertainable basis in fact, that the delay of the three counties in meeting the deadline was substantially due to the secretary's erroneous interpretation of the "error in vote tabulation" requirement.

In their reply brief, Carvin and his colleagues practically ridiculed Boies's interpretation of the law. Noting that the case was controlled by two statutes, one of which says the Election Canvassing Commission *shall* ignore late-filed returns and one of which says the Commission *may* ignore such returns, the Bush brief noted that the Gore lawyers "in contrast, argue that the two statutes together mean that the Commission *can never* ignore late filed returns, but must hold the results of a national election indefinitely pending completion of selective manual recounts in individual counties."[2]

Additionally, the Bush/Carvin brief succinctly addressed the federal issues, first noting that federal law requires states to choose their electors by laws on the books prior to Election Day. Compliance with this provision meant state electors would face no congressional challenge, the so-called "safe harbor" that would later play a prominent role in U.S. Supreme Court deliberations. The brief also made the Due Process and Equal Protection arguments against selective recounts that treat voters in different counties differently "by counting their votes differently depending upon where they reside." The brief also argued that "because the manual recount statute prescribes no meaningful standards for officials conducting such recounts, it permits the invasion of the liberty interest in voting in an arbitrary and capricious manner."

In yet another pre-argument filing, the Bush team's Response in Opposition to (the Gore) Reply brief, the Bush lawyers dealt succinctly with what for them was a nightmare scenario: the possibility that the Court would not only permit the counting to continue, but would accept an invitation in the Boies brief to impose the most liberal counting rules on the county boards. Noting that the issue had not been in the pleadings, the Bush lawyers claimed the Court was without power to decide it, certainly without a separate proceeding to hear evidence and argument on various methods.

The Bush reply brief also warned the Court against pushing the protest deadline too far back, since that would inevitably encroach on the contest litigation. Given the hearings and appeals involved in that process, the Bush brief argued that any counting deadline that extended past November 20 would necessarily impose on the contest period and likely would threaten the safe harbor status so important to the state. Less than three weeks later, the truncated contest period left by the Florida Supreme Court would lead the Supreme Court of the United States to resolve the dispute with finality rather than sending it back to Florida for further proceedings.

At Monday's oral argument, Paul Hancock, a highly capable appellate lawyer, represented the state attorney general's office. Klock represented Secretary Harris. Carvin and Richard argued the case for George W. Bush. From the outset, questions by the Justices betrayed a Court that knew where it wanted to go and sought just a bit of help from the petitioners in getting there. Hancock provided much of that assistance by emphasizing a 1972 U.S. Supreme Court case, *Roudebush v. Hartke*,[3] involving a U.S. Senate contest in Indiana in which the trailing candidate had turned the election around by requesting a recount in just one of the state's ninety-two counties. The Court had affirmed the result, holding that the procedure fell comfortably within the state's constitutional mandate providing for the selection of senators.

The Florida court appreciated that any extension of the recount deadline would necessarily push back the certification date, which in turn triggers the so-called contest period wherein the trailing candidate may challenge the results in court. A truncated contest period could run up against the federal deadline for the certification of Florida's electors. The failure to meet that deadline could strip from the chosen electors their immunity from challenge by the Congress.

So, early in the session Chief Justice Charles Wells asked, "What's the date, the outside date that we're looking at and which puts Florida's votes in jeopardy?"

"December 12, Your Honor, is my understanding," Hancock replied.[4]

From his seat at the counsel bench, Carvin couldn't believe what he was hearing. He had been prepared to make a strong but, in his view, not altogether convincing argument that December 12 was the date by which all disputes had to be resolved, and now here was an opposing counsel making the point for him. If that was the presumed date, the court would have to squeeze both the protest and contest periods into a period of roughly three weeks or cede to the legislature responsibility for picking the electors. Carvin waited to see what Boies would have to say on the subject.

Before Boies argued, Andrew Meyers, representing the Broward County Canvassing Board, appeared briefly to defend a change in counting rules adopted subsequent to the beginning of the count. At first, the board had followed the procedure, which had also governed neighboring Palm Beach County, whereby only hanging chads were counted as votes. But under legal and political pressure exerted by the Gore team, the county had changed midstream to a system that allowed more counter discretion.

This seemed perplexing to Justice Major Harding, who understood the federal admonition against changing the rules after the vote. He asked, "Isn't there something unusual about changing the rules in the middle of the game?"

"I don't think so, Justice Harding," replied Meyers. "I think the important thing is that we do what's right."[5]

Now it was Klock's turn to shake his head. Everyone seemed to want to legislate in this case without even a nod in the direction of federal law, which warns states against changing the rules, on or after election day. "This will never survive appeal," he reflected, as he watched David Boies rise to present his argument.

David Boies has the bearing of a man who believes himself to be just a smidgen smarter than anyone else in the room. This confidence makes him a trifle more forthcoming in dealing with the press, a little less hesitant in exposing his strategy to opposing counsel, and a bit more intuitive in a court of law. He reads the way the court wants to go and manages to find a route to get them there. He studies precedent but appears less bothered by departure from it than many an attorney lacking both his intellectual gifts and self-confidence. Others may worry about defending bad law on appeal. Boies seems to feel his intuition will prevail there too. It is not that he revels in inconsistency; it is simply that he knows the difference between tacking and changing direction.

Boies came out of the chute with a ready-made formula for allowing a court dominated by activist justices to go anywhere they wanted. The seven-day mandatory filing provision? Fine. Make the counties file whatever returns they have compiled by then. But by virtue of a twenty-year-old consent decree with the federal government, the state must count military absentee ballots received up to ten days after the election. So those original returns, "will then be supplemented by manual recounts, by absentee ballots; and then there will be an official return, and that official return will then be certified." Under Boies's reasoning, the only concrete date spelled out by the Florida legislature—the seven-day deadline—becomes just so much wallpaper, totally trumped by a selective recount that, however long it runs, the secretary lacks any discretion to reject.[6]

The chief justice wanted to know whether Boies accepted December 12 as the deadline by which all controversies must be finally determined.

"I do, Your Honor," said Boies.[7]

With that in mind, can the need to meet the December 12 deadline impose some earlier deadline on the protest period recounts?

Boies stated, "I think, Your Honor, you could say . . . that as long as the manual recounts will not impair the [state's ability to determine] the final certification in time to permit the selection of electors by December 12, that those manual recounts must be included."

Justice Barbara Pariente, widely regarded as the paradigm of liberal activism on the bench, asked Boies to address the question of the wide disparity in counting techniques.

Parient asked, "Is the uniformity of how these manual recounts are conducted essential to the integrity of the process or also to the constitutionality of the statute?"

Boies replied, "Your Honor, I think it is important to the integrity of the process. I think if you had very wide variations you could raise constitutional problems."

Boies was less concerned about discrimination against voters in those counties not undergoing recounts because "any candidate could have requested a manual recount in any county."

Returning to the wide disparity in counting methods and again addressing Justice Pariente, Boies urged the Court to take matters into its own hands. "I would say that I think that it, for the reason you point out, it is quite important that this court be as specific as possible in terms of the standard to be applied so that we will have uniformity. I also think, Your Honor, that if you concluded that it was essential to avoid unfairness or some kind of overweighing of one county's vote, this court has within its equitable power to have a statewide recount, if you concluded that that was necessary."[8]

Considering the fact that he and his colleagues were already resigned to a ruling for Gore, Carvin felt the petitioner side of the argument had been a net plus for the Bush case. Boies conceded that December 12 was critical, conceded that differing counting techniques raised serious constitutional issues, and even suggested that to avert the problem of vote dilution in the sixty-three counties not conducting recounts, the Court could decide to invoke its equitable powers to order a statewide recount.

What was Gore up to? Why was he pursuing what Carvin believed to be a risky and lawless strategy, pouring everything into the protest period when an adverse court decision or the failure to win enough votes in the counting process would leave him with a truncated contest period in which to reverse the certified results? Carvin concluded that Gore felt the payoff of plowing into the lead early was so great that he was willing to risk everything to do it. "I always thought the Gore people knew the risks but believed that the Florida Supreme Court would find a way to uphold any lead Gore got and that the U.S. Supreme Court would feel constrained not to overturn the decision of a state court interpreting state law," Carvin later recalled, adding "Another reason, they wanted to take the state legislature out of play. They never thought the legislature would have the guts to undo a Gore victory, as opposed to preserving Bush's certification."

Klock's message to the Court was simple: the seven-day statutory period is not frivolous. Rather it is an essential prerequisite to certification that triggers the contest period when the election outcome can be challenged in the courts and recounts ordered where warranted. Even a dispute about the disqualification of military absentee ballots cannot commence prior to certification. "Once the election is certified, the contest period can begin," argued Klock. "The petitioners are trying to conduct a contest proceeding prior to certification, not for legal reasons, but for political reasons."[9]

Moreover, argued Klock, every legislative indication is that the lawmakers placed a low priority on manual recounts. If a county does not wish to undertake them during the protest period, its discretion is absolute. That was affirmed only two years prior to this election in *Broward County Canvassing Board v. Hogan*,[10] when the state Supreme Court upheld the canvassing board's rejection of a recount request even though the difference between the two candidates was only three votes. As Judge Terry Lewis had found, the Secretary has great discretion to require deadline compliance. In a classic response to the question about the impossibility of completing a recount begun just a day before the deadline, Klock compared that situation to the preparation of a high school term paper. "You can start the term paper the night before, if you want to, but it is unlikely that you'll be able to turn it in the next day when it's due."[11]

To reach a decision for the petitioners, said Klock, would require a vast amount of judicial legislation. The Court would have to do away with the seven-day rule, the protest laws, and the secretary's discretion, "and then the Court enters the great universe of chad to decide, on the record you have, whether or not two corners are enough or three corners are enough."[12]

Klock also noted that there was nothing on the record to suggest that Secretary Harris's views on the question of errors in vote tabulation had delayed any of the counties from proceeding with their recounts.

Carvin faced intense and at times hostile questioning from the bench and enjoyed what was far from his finest day as an appellate lawyer. At one point Justice Pariente seemed to be scolding him for raising parallel questions in the federal courts, asking with a touch of edginess, "You don't think that the state court has it within its jurisdiction to decide whether a statute is being constitutionally applied?"[13]

In response to other questioning, Carvin tried awkwardly to parry questions about the Texas recount statute by protesting that he knew nothing about Texas standards or those of any other state, though such comparisons might have been relevant. He seemed flustered when trying to answer questions on the fate of incomplete manual recounts once the time limit expired.

Carvin had some difficulty arguing on the one hand that recounts in selective counties raised constitutional problems while insisting on the other that Bush had no interest in a broader recount. But he rallied when he told the Court that the matter had been made moot by the passing of the deadline for requesting recounts and that the Court had no power now to revive the issue. "My answer is that anything which departs from the rules that were set before November 7, before the election, by the Florida legislature would be a gross abuse of discretion and impermissible."[14]

In contrast to the judicial slugfest Carvin had endured, Richard was treated with some deference by the bench, permitted first to articulate his theory of the case and then presented with polite, relevant questions. Following closely to the themes laid out in the Bush brief, Richard argued that the Court was being asked to change clear pronouncements by the legislature on the time limit for certification, the discretion of the secretary of state, and the standards for overturning the secretary's decision.

Both the federal and state constitutions, Richard argued, have delegated the power to write election law to the legislature, which in turn delegated certain of those powers to the Secretary. "Now in order for us to do anything else, this court would have to disregard the most fundamental principles of separation of powers and do what these appellants are asking, to step into the shoes of both the legislative and the executive branches, to rewrite these statutes, and to begin the process, which I suggest to this court is never-ending, of sitting as a determiner or an ultimate arbiter of the minutiae of facts that go into the election process."[15]

What about the Boies notion of serial certifications as the recounts came in? Boies stated, "The suggestion by appellants that there can be continuous certifications and supplement certifications is not what the statute says. If you'll read the statute, it says there is one certification mandated by 5 P.M. seven days after the election and that's the only one."[16] Only the military ballots can come three days later, and that is a function of federal law, which is binding, on Florida.

At the Bush headquarters, low expectations were mixed with some anguish for Carvin's tough afternoon. Baker had watched the session closely and felt that Richard's fine performance was due in part to his own skills and in part to the Court's deference to a fellow Floridian. Richard, he and Ginsberg decided, should be the constant in all state court trials and arguments, playing a starring role in the most important arguments and little more than a cameo role in the lesser disputes. This decision did not sit well with many of the legal eagles grinding out briefs and talking points for the frontline advocates or battling Gore's shock troops in the recount trenches. To them, Richard was something of a legal dandy, glib and smooth, but not terribly studious and occasionally prone to inexplicably exclude a leading case or point of law. He was a hired-gun Democrat and they were true-believing Republicans. They resented his relatively short ten-hour work-days because they sweltered round-the-clock, and they resented his daily presence at Tallahassee's finer eateries while they gulped cold cheeseburgers from paper bags. They resented his Boies-like appearances on national television while they were cultivating the sort of contempt for the liberal media they would need to get along in a Bush administration. On one occasion, Richard's participation in a staff discussion of an upcoming case was interrupted when his media man appeared to announce that it was time to leave for Larry King Live. Were mental images translatable into reality, Richard might well have been found later that evening dangling from a tree by a pair of garish suspenders.

On November 21, in a unanimous per curium opinion, the Florida Supreme Court ruled for Gore. Secretary Harris's interpretation of the term "error in vote tabulation" was wrong, the Court held. The Court adopted Boies's formulation of seperating manual recounts from the seven-day statutory deadline. Further, the Court found that the secretary had extremely limited discretion to disallow manual recount results, whenever completed:

> We conclude that, consistent with the Florida election scheme, the Secretary may reject a Board's amended returns only if the returns are submitted so late that their inclusion will preclude a candidate from contesting the certification or preclude Florida's voters from participating fully in the federal electoral process.[17]

This was an extremely strange bit of lawmaking. Why ask the secretary to determine on an ad hoc basis, when extend-

ing the protest period will unduly constrict the contest period, when that judgment had already been made in the most
concrete way by the legislature that had established the deadlines in the first place? The answer seems to be that the legislative formula did not produce the results desired by the
Court, so it set about to rewrite that formula. In the end, of
course, it was this judicial revision of the law that would lay
waste to the contest period, leaving the vice president and his
supporters feeling cheated. For this predicament, the Florida
Supreme Court must bear substantial responsibility.

Having decided to ignore the statutory timetable, the
Court searched hard for a colorable pretext. It found two
Florida provisions that, it concluded, rendered the seven-day
requirement ambiguous. One involved the recount laws
identified by Judge Lewis, which could give the canvassing
boards only a day to conduct their recounts. The second was
a provision fining members of the board $200 apiece for
each day's delay beyond the seven-day deadline. Were the
late recount results to be excluded, said the Court, the canvassing board would have no reason to submit them, thus
incurring a fine, so the provisions for such fines would be
meaningless. Even by the elastic standards of this particular
Court, this represented a stretch. Suppose, for example, that
the board, through laziness or negligence files the returns
three days late. The secretary, in her discretion, could well
decide to accept the late-filed returns and enforce fines to-
taling $600 against each member. There simply was no con-
flict save that invented by the Court itself.

Although the court paid lip service to legislative intent as
the "polestar" guiding its decision, the court paid considerable attention to Florida constitutional provisions exalting
the right to vote. But having made a hash of the election laws
passed by the legislature, the Court declined to suggest new
dates or timetables. "We decline to rule more expansively,
for to do so would result in this Court substantially rewriting the Code. We leave that matter to the sound discretion of
the body best equipped to address it—the Legislature."[18]

What then to do about the chaos now that not a single legislative provision or executive prerogative was left standing? Any action by the court might be considered legislating from the bench in contravention of federal law. "Because of our reluctance to rewrite the Florida Election Code," wrote the demure Justices, "we conclude that we must invoke the equitable powers of this Court to fashion a remedy that will allow a fair and expeditious resolution of the questions presented here."[19]

The Court established Sunday, November 26, at 5 P.M. as the new deadline for filing amended certifications, provided the secretary's office was open. If not, the deadline would be 9 A.M. on Monday, November 27. The justices said nothing about appropriate counting standards, but they cited with approval the words of the Illinois Supreme Court in the 1990 case of *Pullen v. Mulligan*,[20] which concluded that slavish devotion to any means of tabulating votes should yield to the effort to interpret the intent of the individual voter. Indeed, "where the intention of the voter can be fairly and satisfactorily ascertained, that intention should be given effect," the Illinois court ruling stated. In Palm Beach County, Boies would try unsuccessfully to use *Pullen* as a bludgeon in order to force the liberal counting of dimpled chads.

That the decision had been anticipated at Bush headquarters in Tallahassee made it no less painful. The counting practices in the three remaining counties had taken on a circus quality, and there was no way of predicting what numbers might be produced. Gore was winning on the political front and on both the state and federal legal fronts. To add insult to injury, the Florida Supreme Court had thrown in a footnote quoting Judge Middlebrooks's salute to manual recounts from the case lost just a week previously.

Tired and bitter, Baker, for the first time since his arrival in Tallahassee, looked his age as he read a statement attacking the Court's decision:

> Today, Florida's Supreme Court rewrote the legislature's statutory system, assumed the responsibilities of the Executive branch, and sidestepped the opinion of the trial court as the finder of fact.

Two weeks after the election, that Court has changed the rules and invented a new system for counting the election results. One should not now be surprised if the Florida Legislature seeks to affirm the original rules.[21]

Many commentators would find Baker's remarks intemperate, but to the sullen, deflated crowd at state GOP headquarters they struck a welcome tone of pluck and resistance. As he strode back into the building, Baker received a long standing ovation.

The Baker team still had an important decision to make: whether or not to file a writ of certiorari asking the U.S. Supreme Court to review the Florida decision. Once again, Baker, Ginsberg, Olson, Terwilliger, Zoellick, and Josh Bolten gathered to discuss the options. Olson saw only a 35 to 40 percent chance the court would take the case, though if it did, he reasoned the chances of prevailing were better than 50 percent. He liked the case already in the federal courts better, although just days earlier the court of appeals for the eleventh circuit had declined to overturn Judge Middlebrook's decision denying immediate relief. Like Middlebrooks, the appellate court had expressly deferred to the State of Florida, which it held should be given the first shot at adjudicating the matters raised by Bush. Still, Olson felt that the issues in that case were cleaner, there was less interpretation of state law involved, and there was no need for reversal of the state courts. Others saw the legislature as the best hope and thought a rush to the U.S. Supreme Court would cloud that option, particularly if the legislature joined the case. They asked: What could we expect from the U.S. Supreme Court? It will probably take a week or ten days to get a decision, even if they grant the petition. By then the recounts will be history. Certification will have taken place. If Gore has won, will the court take away his votes? And if they do, won't he get them right back in the contest period?

But Baker, Terwilliger, and Ginsberg took an insistent stance: This is a multi-front war and it must be fought everywhere at once. This is no time to get squeamish. What the

Florida court did was so brazen, it's hard to believe that the U.S. Supreme Court would let it stand. Besides, don't ever think of the Florida legislature as the final arbiter to this campaign. If we're ahead as December 12 approaches, they may confirm our victory. But if Gore is certified by then, it's questionable what they can or will do. And it's also questionable if Bush will want a state legislature to place him in the White House after he's lost the national popular vote and the vote in Florida, however it's counted.

Once again the decision to go federal was made in Tallahassee, and once again the folks in Austin-Crawford confirmed it.

Baker thought about the period immediately ahead. Not too much was going to be happening in the courts in the next five days. The action was plainly in Miami-Dade, Broward, and Palm Beach counties. That's where the presidency could be lost; that's where the ground war must be won.

CHAPTER 4

Fighting the Ground War

From the moment Al Gore first requested recounts in four selected counties, the optimal Bush-Baker goal was to stop the recounts in the state or federal courts. Failing that, the Florida legislature was a potential trump card, but that looked much better on paper than in practice because the legislature could do very little before December 12, by which time developments on other fronts might well have pre-empted its realistic choices. The third necessary prong of the Baker strategy was to fight the ground war on recounts. This meant getting the most restrictive counting rules possible, keeping an eye on the counters to make sure the standards were being enforced, preparing to do battle in the local courts when the Gore team sought to change the recount rules, and mobilizing a presence in the state of outside political heavyweights to lean on local officials. The overwhelming need, Baker explained to his legal minions time and again, was to prevent Gore from pulling ahead. Gore being in the lead changes everything: the national political picture, the federal legal context, and the situation with the state courts and the Florida legislature.

This strategy meant playing defense, and as had been evident from the first machine recount, there are advantages to being on the attack in terms of picking both the issues and the venues. Gore had gotten off to a running start because of the butterfly ballot problem in Palm Beach County. By midafternoon of Election Day, the DNC had retained TeleQuest, an Oklahoma-based telemarketing firm, to generate some mischief. Voters called were urged to vote for Gore. But the message continued: "If you have already voted and think you may have punched the wrong hole for the incorrect candidate, you should return to the polls and request that the election officials write down your name so that this problem can be fixed."[1]

The following day Jesse Jackson stormed into Florida charging that voting irregularities had cost Gore a clear win. He would join forces in the state with Kweisi Mfume, president of the NAACP, who promptly convened hearings designed to show that African-Americans had been systematically disenfranchised, and with Rabbi Steven Jacobs of Kol Tikvah Temple in Los Angeles, an old Jackson ally. Jackson led marches and addressed rallies in Miami, Fort Lauderdale, and Palm Beach. Directing one pitch to Jewish people, whom he once referred to as "Hymies," Jackson cried, "Once again, the sons and daughters of slavery and Holocaust survivors are bound together by their hopes and their fear about national public policy."[2]

"We must stand together or we will perish alone," Jacobs chimed in, in what must surely have been the most overblown rhetoric ever provoked by a butterfly ballot.[3]

In fact, charges of civil rights depredations would shadow the Florida contest, surviving to the January 6 ceremonial counting of electoral votes, where members of the Congressional Black Caucus sought unsuccessfully to delay the event, and even beyond, as the United States Commission on Civil Rights took its own jaundiced look at Florida. One by one the charges of official racism evaporated even in the light of evidence the Commission chose to consider. For example, a police roadblock, allegedly designed to intimidate African-Americans and keep them away from the polls, turned out to be a routine spot check for driver's licenses at a site roughly equidistant from one predominantly black polling station and one predominantly white one, and which resulted in more citations issued to white drivers. Also, charges of multiple identification checks of black voters were shown to have been attributable to occasional confusion resulting from clerical error.

By contrast, a December 1, 2000 report in the Miami Herald based on a review of 5,000 ballots cast in twelve Florida counties indicated that at least 445 convicted felons had voted illegally, and as many as 5,000 may have done so statewide. Of the 445 illegal ballots, 75 percent had been cast by registered Democrats, including sixty-two robbers, fifty-six drug dealers, forty-five killers, sixteen rapists, and seven kidnappers.

Baker was concerned that decisions would be made under political mob influence. He talked to Enright and others about some Republican counterweight. Slowly, pro-Bush Floridians were assembled at various nerve points in the recount battle. Republican congressional staffers and others flown in from out of town to keep the vigil would augment their numbers.

Of the three remaining counties selected by Gore for recounts, two—Broward and Miami-Dade—decided at first not to proceed. Broward, using the "hanging chad" standard endorsed ten years earlier by Theresa LePore in Palm Beach County, turned up only four additional net Gore votes after sampling some 4,000 ballots. On November 13 the canvassing board voted 2–1 against a broad recount. Judge Robert Lee, the chairman and a Democrat, explained that he had cast his "no" vote on the basis of the director of elections's opinion that "errors in vote tabulation" did not embrace voter mistakes. The following day, however, with the Butterworth advisory opinion contradicting Harris-Roberts, and with Democrats threatening to take the majority Democrat board to court, Judge Lee reconsidered, joining Democrat Suzanne Gunzburger in voting "yes." Jane Carroll, the lone Republican on the board, voted against reconsideration. She would resign on November 21, to be replaced by Judge Robert Rosenberg, the Republican whose earnest squinting search with a magnifying glass for light at the end of the chad would turn him into a national emblem signifying the folly of the procedure.

However, when it began its recount on November 15, the Broward board adopted an objective standard, counting "hanging" or "swinging" chads—those with at least two corners detached—but not "pregnant" or "dimpled" chads, which showed bulges or indentations, but still had all four corners attached. According to Judge Lee, "We did it at the advice of the county attorney so that no one could say later we were trying to guess back and forth was that a vote, was it not a vote."[4]

Baker sent Mike Madigan, an experienced Washington hand, who had served as chief counsel to Senator Fred Thompson's special committee investigating campaign fundraising abuses, to represent Bush's interests in Broward County. Madigan knew that the absentee ballot count would likely double or triple Bush's 300-vote lead and that after Miami, Broward, and Palm Beach, Gore had nowhere else to go for votes. So Madigan figured the Democrats would pull out all stops to bolster the Gore vote in Broward. On November 17, the Democrats sued in the circuit court, asking Judge John A. Miller to order the counting of dimpled and pregnant chads. Boies appeared and maintained that Broward should adopt the same liberal standard followed by Massachusetts in the 1996 *Delahunt v. Johnson*[5] case and Illinois in the 1990 *Pullen v. Mulligan* case. Both, said Boies, had recognized the dimpled chad as a valid vote. To underline the point, he presented an affidavit from an Illinois lawyer, Michael E. Lavelle, who represented Ms. Pullen in the case, to describe the decision in which at least some dimpled chads were counted.

Both cases fell short of being dispositive of the issue. *Delahunt* involved a special primary election with only a single contest on the ballot, thus negating the notion that a voter would come to the polls but choose not to vote in one particular election. Yet 22 percent of the ballots were blank in some precincts. Why? Delahunt told the *Washington Post* that a severe thunderstorm the day of the vote had left many ballots soggy and hard to punch through.[6]

The *Pullen* decision did not hold that dimpled chads must be counted, simply that visual inspection of ballots to discern voter intention in cases where the tabulating machine had failed to count them was appropriate, and that the court below should examine each ballot for voter intent rather than exclude entire classes of ballots, such as those where the chad was not at least partially detached. A close reading of both the Lavelle affidavit and the Illinois decision does not support the allegation that either Lavelle or Boies misled the Court, any more than it supports the claim that under Pullen, all dimpled chads must be counted. Indeed, both Broward and Palm Beach counties may each have thought they were applying the Pullen standard, but they ended up establishing sharply different evidentiary standards for interpreting voter intent. The difference between the 1990 Illinois race and the 2000 Florida race was simply that the former involved a single state legislative district while the latter involved sixty-four state counties, each with the potential, while adhering to the same general standard, to interpret that standard in vastly different ways.

In Broward, canvassing board chairman Lee, who often seemed to be more at the mercy of events than in control of them, was candid about what was at stake. "If we are required to change the procedure of evaluating the ballot, there are clearly literally going to be hundreds of more votes in this county that will be counted," he said. "In all likelihood, the majority of those will go to Al Gore. And I want that to be clear."[7] Judge Miller stopped short of issuing the order sought by Gore, but made on-the-record comments suggesting a broader standard. Clearly, the counters were now able to do a bit of freelancing.

"They changed the rules so they could manufacture additional votes for Gore," charged Montana Governor Racicot. "It is wrong, it is flawed, and it is a process that is simply and quite honestly not worthy of our democracy."[8]

Madigan was having problems even apart from the counting standard. He saw hundreds of counters and observers "manhandling ballots." He observed chads "all over tables, all over the floor." Other GOP observers watched one Democrat eat two chads and another stuff one in her pocket. Madigan protested one instance where a group of eighty absentee ballots arrived with the Bush chad punched through but taped over and the Gore chads cleanly punched through. Madigan suspected that the Democrats wanted to "generate enough confusion to create 3,000 challenged ballots." After counting about 55,000 ballots in the Government Hurricane Center, the board decided to repair to the county courthouse and continue the counting in the context of a formal meeting. The change represented more than terminology. At a meeting, Florida's sunshine laws apply less sternly. This allowed the board to bar speakers and truncate arguments, permitting only observers.

On November 19, Broward County Attorney Andrew J. Meyers, fresh from his Supreme Court argument on behalf of Gore, advised the board that its standards were "impermissibly narrow," and that the board must "determine the clear intent of each ballot whenever that intent can be determined." He added that it would be "problematic to articulate specific parameters" in determining whether to count a vote.[9] The Board then changed the rules in the middle of the recount and decided to review the undervotes, which had failed to pass the previous "hanging" or "swinging" chad test. Still, no one seemed able to articulate the new standard, least of all Chairman Lee. On November 22, he said, "It's not objectively subjective or subjectively objective, but I think it's somewhere in the middle. It's not a whim."[10]

Madigan and another Bush lawyer, Patrick Oxford, had by now moved from disaster prevention mode to calamity prevention mode. They went to court on Thanksgiving Day, still arguing over standards, and got into a near shouting match with Gore's lawyers over the Pullen case affidavit. Tallahassee sent Governor Marc Racicot of Montana to Broward, where he demanded to address the board on the counting issue. When Madigan sought to make a record of his objections at the meeting, Lee threatened to have him thrown out. Lee ordered police to expel GOP attorney Bill Scherer for repeated objections to the counting of dimpled chads.

"Am I under arrest?" Scherer demanded.

"No," was the reply.

"Then take your hands off me."

They did, but after lunch Judge Lee did not permit Scherer to return to the counting room.

As the counting proceeded, Democrat Gunzburger appeared never to see a dimple she couldn't interpret, Republican Rosenberg sought to apply the two-corner rule wherever possible, and Judge Lee seemed to go in whatever direction caprice suggested.

By November 25, Baker was desperate and increasingly pessimistic. Not only was the counting going badly, but MSNBC was reporting—erroneously, it turned out—that 500 new absentee ballots from Israel had showed up in Broward County. "Broward is killing us," Baker complained. "They're going to steal the election." He decided to pour celebrities into the breach. Broward could soon boast more political elders than a Chinese strategy session on Tiananmen Square. Bob Dole and Governors Christie Todd Whitman of New Jersey, Frank Keating of Oklahoma, and John Engler of Michigan were among those who came to the Broward counting room to bear witness to the debacle and convey the unfairness to a perplexed nation.

"They've gone from counting votes to looking for votes to now manufacturing votes," complained Representative John E. Sweeney, a New York Republican.[11]

"I literally can't sleep over this," remarked Governor George Pataki of New York, another Broward visitor. "I have never been as appalled in my life. It really makes me disillusioned with government. How can you hour by hour change the rules to try to come up with the right results? This is not something you do in America."[12]

There was yet another reason for the parade of notables. "We were tracking everything on our computers," Madigan later recalled. "The presence of celebrities negatively influenced the discovery of new votes. Even Gunzburger didn't find Gore votes at the same rate when Christie Whitman was in the room. We decided, with celebrities around they cheat less."

Still, Gore gained 567 net votes in Broward. If he could have matched that in Palm Beach or Miami-Dade, the Bush lead would have evaporated, and Florida would have been Gore's to lose.

Madigan, Oxford, and others returned to Tallahassee to organize their records in preparation for future litigation. "We knew there was going to be a contest," Terwilliger later recalled. "What we didn't know was whether we would be playing offense or defense."

Two weeks later, Phil Beck, Bush's lead attorney in the contest lawsuit, would decide against putting the Broward evidence before Judge Sanders Sauls. "It was a strong case, but my judgment was we didn't need it." Beck later recalled. "The Gore case had been so weak, I just wanted to get the trial over and get out of there."

If the Broward results failed to send the Gore team into paroxysms of joy, the reason was that it contained the lone good news among the three counties in play. Palm Beach had adopted a counting system that was generating new votes with only 8 percent of the ballots, compared to 24 percent in Broward County. And Miami had stopped counting altogether, its canvassing board coming to the unanimous conclusion that it could not complete even a truncated and probably illegal count of some 10,500 undervotes by the court-imposed deadline.

MIAMI-DADE

Baker and Ginsberg sent Bobby Burchfield, general counsel for the 1992 Bush reelection campaign, to fight Gore's recount in Miami-Dade County. Burchfield thought the task would be difficult. "It's O.K. to attack in a state like Florida, but it is very hard to defend," he later recalled. "It was imperative that we always stay up because we felt the media would turn on us the moment we fell behind."

But Miami-Dade was far from the bleakest battleground in the state for Bush. For one thing, the county vote had been rather close, 53–46 for Gore, nothing like the landslide margins in Palm Beach and Broward Counties. This limited somewhat Gore's potential for a big vote pickup in the manual recount, regardless of the counting system used. Another key asset was the large, predominantly Republican Cuban community. Forty years in the country, a powerful force in Florida politics, and with its sense of outrage and activism freshly stoked by the Elian Gonzalez affair, "Little Havana" could provide able and sophisticated attorneys to help in the battle and, if necessary, spirited groups to take their campaign to the streets. Miguel De Grandy, a partner in Greenberg Traurig, and former U.S. Attorney Roberto Martinez were already on hand, ready to do battle. And the Democrats were far from united. Blacks, Jews, and non-Cuban Hispanics did not always speak with a single voice and frequently had trouble organizing and executing a cohesive political strategy. Finally, the canvassing board itself held some promise. De Grandy and Rodriguez held out little hope for Judge Lawrence King, the chairman, whom they regarded as a partisan Democrat, but Democrats Miriam Lehr, and David Leahy, the county supervisor of elections, were given to episodic attacks of reason.

The Democrats started slowly, first requesting a recount and then withdrawing the request, substituting instead the request to manually recount only the undervotes. On November 14, the original deadline for certification, the board finally moved to conduct a sample recount in three precincts representing three percent of the total vote that had gone for Gore by margins approaching or exceeding 9–1. Prior to initiating that recount, the board rejected Leahy's proposal to adopt a two-corner counting standard, preferring to make judgments of voter intentions on the fly. Despite such lax standards, the net Gore pickup was only six votes. Leahy argued that the change did not show an "error in the vote tabulation sufficient to change the result," and that no reasonable extrapolation could indicate a potential change sufficient to affect the election results. With Judge King dissenting, Leahy and Lehr, on November 14, voted 2–1 against proceeding with a full manual recount. The board voted 3–0 against simply counting undervotes, concluding that the act would violate Florida law, which in cases of manual recounts mandates the counting of all ballots. Al Gore promptly denounced the decision.

After meeting with the board on the evening of November 15 to urge reconsideration of the decision, local Democratic officials contacted Lehr the following day and urged her to resign so she could be replaced with a more dependable partisan, Miami-Dade Commissioner Gwen Margolis. Lehr declined to walk that plank, but at a meeting on November 17 to reconsider the earlier decision, she joined forces with King, providing a 2–1 margin for initiating the recount. She claimed she was influenced by the hefty Gore totals that had been or were being run up in Volusia and Broward counties.

During the next few days, the board seemed confused as to whether to begin counting all votes or simply the undervotes. Martinez and Rodriguez filed a lawsuit seeking to block the counting, but the circuit court dismissed the suit, saying the issues were already before the state supreme court. On November 19, the board ran the ballots through machines designed to scrape away hanging chads and separate undervotes. It also decided 2–1, with Leahy again dissenting, to count "rogue dimples," where the presidential contest alone was marked by a dimpled or pregnant chad. The counting itself began on November 20, six days after the statutory deadline for certified returns to be filed. The following day the Florida Supreme Court approved the manual recounts, but also established the November 26 deadline.

That night the board held a meeting with representatives of the Bush and Gore teams. Despite twenty-five counting tables that had been organized on the eighteenth floor of the Stephen P. Clark Government Center, the board estimated that it would take until early December to complete the recount. Burchfield predicted that it would take longer than that.

Sensing weakness and concerned that they had been out-manned and out-demonstrated up to that point, the Republicans struck back. Baker asked two congressmen, Lincoln Diaz-Belart of Florida and John Sweeney of New York, to attend the next day's counting session. Republican telephone banks were urging party members to go to the Government Center the following morning to protest the count. Radio Mambi, the leading Spanish-language radio station in the area, urged Cuban-American Republicans to demonstrate. Newly arrived Washington staffers were ready for deployment. GOP observers could man every counting table on the floor and then some. Mehlman, moving bodies from his Miami base, was showing an extraordinary flair for logistics.

Early on November 22, the board announced that it could not complete the manual recount by the court deadline. Instead, it proposed moving from the eighteenth to the nineteenth floor to tabulate only the 10,750 undervotes.

Burchfield protested heatedly. The applicable law requires the counting of all ballots once a manual recount was started and makes no provision for isolating overvotes, undervotes, or any other single category. Moreover, the nineteenth floor provided smaller areas, one able to accommodate only two observers from each side, and no media. Reporters from the *New York Times*, the *Wall Street Journal*, and CNN and others complained bitterly that the new arrangement violated Florida's Sunshine Law (which requires opening most government proceedings to the public); they circulated a petition protesting the action, implicitly threatening a lawsuit. Most offended were the GOP observers who had been divided among the twenty-five counting tables; they were now threatened with expulsion. Augmented by Washington "imports," a few dozen took up positions outside the new counting facility and began chanting "let us in" and "no justice, no peace." Outside, a crowd briefly surrounded Joe Geller, the Miami-Dade Democratic chairman, and accused him of stealing a ballot. He was not touched and was escorted from the scene by police. Upstairs, the *New York Times* would report that "several people were trampled, punched or kicked when protesters tried to rush the doors outside the office of the Miami-Dade supervisor of elections."[13] The report was exaggerated; there were no confirming witness accounts and no evidence of any injuries.

At 1:30 P.M. the board reconvened on the eighteenth floor and announced that its members were unable to complete even the tabulation of undervotes by the November 26 deadline. They asked for comments. At the time they stopped, the board had counted in what was essentially a north-south direction and had completed Precincts 101 through 137, situated along the heavily Jewish Gold Coast, and Precincts 138 through 200 in the predominantly African-American sections of Miami. Only five of the 199 Cuban-American community precincts had been counted and most of the affluent Republican pockets north of Miami had not been counted at all. Altogether, 139 precincts had been manually recounted, about 20 percent of the Miami-Dade total, with much of the rest in areas that had supported George W. Bush. Nor was it entirely clear what standard, if any, the board had used. Leahy seemed to adopt some form of two-corner standard but King seemed to feel that if it's on the ballot and near the Gore hole, it's a vote. Lehr was somewhere in between. Altogether the canvassing board was finding recoverable votes in about 22 percent of the undervotes, compared to 26 percent in Broward County and 8 percent in Palm Beach.

In that context, the 168 votes Gore had picked up under counting rules that maximized his potential were not particularly impressive, and the opinions of vote projection experts in both camps would be that Gore would gain little, and could even lose votes, were the process to be resumed where it left off. In response to the call for comments, De Grandy argued that should the board decide to suspend its vote count, it must wipe the slate clean, because to count only those precincts from heavily Democratic areas would not only distort the Miami-Dade results, but could also violate the 1965 Voting Rights Act in that it would discriminate against Cuban-Americans, a protected group. De Grandy further argued that counting under-votes alone runs contrary to statutory law.

Jack Scott, one of the Democratic lawyers, replied that the real problem in the Votomatic™ machine districts involved undervotes and that counting them alone was the best available solution at this point in time.

With the issue still under discussion, a breathless Marc Racicot raced into the room, found Burchfield and asked, "Bobby, are they going to shut this thing down?"

"I'm not sure, wait and see," replied Burchfield.

At 2:15 P.M. the board announced its decision. By a 3–0 vote it had decided to cease counting. There was no way to meet the deadline and still count all the votes. And counting just the undervotes would not be worth the effort because it was probably illegal.

The predominantly Republican audience roared its approval. Democratic representatives announced that they would seek a writ of mandamus from the courts. Baker was at the other end of Burchfield's cell phone. "Respond to whatever they do in court," he barked. "This is the whole ball game."

Gore filed a writ of mandamus in the Third District Court of Appeals at 8 P.M. The Bush response, largely prepared by Joel Kaplan, a former law clerk to Justice Antonin Scalia, was in by 8:15 P.M.

At 9:30 P.M. the Gore motion was denied. Although the court found the canvassing board had a "mandatory duty to re-count all of the ballots in the county," it found no way it could do so in the allotted time and thus declined to order a futile act. "Twenty-four hours earlier we had just been hammered by the Florida Supreme Court," Burchfield later recalled. "Twenty-four hours later we were virtually euphoric about our position."

On Thanksgiving Day, Gore attorneys filed a writ of mandamus with the Florida Supreme Court asking that it order the Miami-Dade Canvassing Board to resume the count. Burchfield, Kaplan, and Rodriguez went to work on a response, hoping to have it in by 3:30 P.M. At 3:15, the state Supreme Court denied the writ without waiting for the response but "without prejudice" for Gore to raise the issue at a future point.

Democrats would try to exploit the circumstances surrounding the board's decision to suspend the count. Board members assured one and all they had not been intimidated by the demonstrations of those locked out on the nineteenth floor. Yet the notion that a small band of protesting vote-count observers and congressional staff troubadours could hijack the American democracy was peddled with a vengeance. Representative Jerrold Nadler from New York proclaimed that "the whiff of fascism is in the air."[14] And Senator Joseph Lieberman, who probably knew better, gravely warned against the tactics of pressure and intimidation.

On February 26, 2001, the *Miami Herald* reported on the results of its reexamination of the 10,644 ballots that the Miami-Dade election office had identified as undervotes. Using the most liberal counting rules—pregnant and dimpled chads counting as votes—Gore would have picked up a net forty-nine votes, not enough when combined with Broward and Palm Beach counties to reverse Bush's victory in the state and, hence, the Electoral College. Using more conservative standards, Bush's lead would actually have increased.

PALM BEACH

John Bolton, an American Enterprise Institute scholar and former law partner at Covington and Burling, was at a conference in Korea when he began getting word of the problems in Florida. He called Baker and asked if he could help. A week later, he was in Palm Beach County leading the Bush effort at damage control. The great court battles were being fought at another level, but here in the trenches, Bolton thought, was where the outcome in Florida could well be decided.

The Palm Beach County Canvassing Board agreed promptly to Gore's request for a sample recount. As the home of Theresa LePore's 1990 guidance for judging chads as votes, the Bush team had every reason to expect that standard to be enforced. Instead, the board periodically resorted to "sunshine" tests—counting any punctured chad through which light could be seen as a vote. Then it would switch back to the 1990 standard, and possibly switch again to where at least one counter, Democrat Carol Roberts, appeared to be viewing dimpled chads as countable votes. When the board completed its sample, Gore had picked up nineteen votes. Even allowing for the overwhelmingly Democratic sympathies of the selected counties, Bolton, Baker, and others working for Bush feared that Gore could use Palm Beach to finally elbow his way into the lead. Their concerns were heightened on November 12 when the board decided on a second automated recount. Bolton later claimed that hundreds of chads were separated from ballots by the counting devices.

Clearly the Gore camp sensed that something significant could happen in Palm Beach. Just as in their amended Florida Supreme Court brief they had asked the court to order the counting of dimpled chads, here they made the same request on November 15 before a circuit court judge, Jorge Labarga. That same day Judge Labarga held that "the present policy utilized by the local election officials restricts the canvassing board's ability to determine the intent of the voter. . . . To that end, the present policy of a per se exclusion of any ballot that does not have a partially punched or hanging chad, is not in compliance with the law."[15] He stopped short of requiring the board to consider dimpled or pregnant chads, leaving it to Judge Charles E. Burton and his colleagues to work things out.

Bolton understood that the substantive changes in procedure could well become an issue in the federal litigation. But he recognized that his mission was more to achieve the most favorable outcome on the ground than to build a record for future lawsuits. The overall optimal strategy was to kill the recounts. The local strategy was to get the best standard possible. To that end, on November 16, Bolton met with Burton, LePore, Roberts, and county attorney Denise Dietrich, urging that Palm Beach resist the temptation to speculate regarding voter intent and instead stay as close as possible to the original LePore standards. "These ex parte contacts with the voting officials were important," Bolton later recalled. He was a partisan. Everyone knew that. But if he could also be viewed as a problem solver, his opinions with the board would carry some weight.

Counting in Palm Beach County began on the night of Wednesday, November 16. On some days as many as thirty counting stations were set up at the Emergency Operation Center. Metal boxes containing the results of between one and five precincts were divided up among the counting teams. No single standard applied, but at the initial stage Bolton did not regard this with too much concern because Republican observers were on hand to protest any decision they found unreasonable. By agreement, these challenged or questionable ballots were set aside for later consideration by the canvassing board itself.

On Saturday, when the board started to examine the questionable ballots, Burton called his fellow members together along with representatives of the two camps. After some back and forth, Burton said he thought he had come up with a reasonable standard. On the Palm Beach County ballots, voters were called upon to make twenty-five decisions. Clearly, a single dimple was probative of nothing. Any effort to place it in one column or another would be more speculation than interpretation. But suppose a voter had ten dimples on his ballot, or even five? Most likely that voter thought he was casting a ballot when he simply manipulated his stylus through the hole, or he perhaps lacked the physical strength to vote correctly by punching the stylus though the hole until the chad was dislodged. Burton proposed that in a race where the voter had left dimples on at least 20 percent of his ballots, an effort should be made to interpret his preference. Where the dimples appeared on fewer than 20 percent, the dimple should be ignored.

Burton got his way, although Bolton came to believe that LePore in her counting was applying a somewhat stricter standard than Burton, and Roberts continued to find votes when she saw light at the end of the chad. But if Bolton was not 100 percent certain what standards were being applied, he knew they were anathema to the Democrats who were failing to gain anything like the votes they had expected after the sample precinct recount.

On November 21, the Democrats filed a "Motion for Clarification" before Judge Labarga asking him to issue an injunction against the counting board, requiring them to consider the "totality of circumstances" as regards voter intent with respect to each ballot, and to "count indentations as votes, absent other evidence on the face of the ballot that clearly indicates a voter's intention to abstain or vote for another candidate." To the Baker team this was shaping up as the potentially decisive struggle. The state Supreme Court that day had swept Katherine Harris aside and extended the recount deadline until November 26. The Miami-Dade recount was in full swing. Broward had clearly gone "haywire" and was manufacturing votes for Gore about as fast as they came out of the box. "If we can't stop the hemorrhage in Palm Beach, we can lose this recount," Baker told Bolton.

"We saw this as the battle for Stalingrad," Bolton later recalled. "If we lost here they would just roll over us."

To Bolton's consternation, Baker and Ginsberg dispatched Barry Richard to Palm Beach to argue the case. In descending order of magnitude, Bolton was contemptuous of Democrats, trial lawyers, and media hogs, and he saw Richard as having hit the trifecta. Plus, he knew the case and the personalities well by now and felt with typical lawyer's pride that he was best situated to argue to the court. But when he heard definitively from Tallahassee that it was not to be, he played the good soldier and urged Richard to do what he would have done: put Burton on the stand and let him relate "judge to judge" to Labarga over what the business of counting was all about.

Richard did precisely that the following day. On November 22, Burton, questioned by county attorney Dietrich, patiently explained that he was trying to apply the standard Labarga had established the previous week and that his method was as fair as any could be, but it was not rigid. No one on the board would be impervious to clear evidence of voter intent.

As a way of emphasizing the fact that many dimples could not be correctly interpreted as votes, Burton brought to court one of the Votomatic machines used in the county and tried to create dimples by lightly touching the chads. As he would later testify at the contest trial, "It was very difficult for me to make an indentation like that, because it was quite easy for me to pop out the chad."[16]

Once again, Judge Labarga, in his order, reminded the board that "each ballot must be considered in light of the totality of the circumstances," and reminded Burton and his colleagues that they "cannot have a policy in place of per se exclusion of any ballot." But he failed to issue the injunction sought by the Gore team and, if anything, paid greater deference than in his earlier order to the discretion vested in the canvassing boards by the state legislature.[17] Burton and his colleagues treated the Labarga order as vindicating their approach and urging them to continue with no change in their ground rules.

Unable to impose their counting rules in Palm Beach County, the Gore team faced the even bleaker prospect that the canvassing board there might miss the November 26 deadline imposed by the Supreme Court. "At the nitty gritty level the new date was bad for the Democrats," Bolton later recalled. "When Miami-Dade stopped, the world began to see that the recount strategy would produce no big victory for Al Gore."

Despite the time crunch, Burton and his colleagues decided to take Thanksgiving Day off, a bewildering decision to many participants in the battle and members of the media, but not to the county workers who had been working sixteen to eighteen hour days and could only look forward to worse as the deadline approached. Gore himself announced on the holiday that he would be contesting the official tally, the kind of challenge never before launched in a presidential campaign and a sure sign that he had given up the belief that his selective recount strategy would block Bush's certification. Still the Gore lawyers pressed on. On November 24, they tried again to make the case, this time before the canvassing board itself, that the wrong standards were being applied, but they got nowhere. With the deadline just hours away, the Gore pickup in Palm Beach County barely exceeded 150 votes, far from the giddy numbers projected after the one-percent sample.

Still, the Bush team had to remain alert. In the rush to have the job done by 5 P.M., corners were cut. Suddenly Palm Beach counters stopped segregating objected-to ballots for final decision by the three-person board; some seventy precincts escaped such scrutiny.

At 3 P.M. on November 26, Burton placed a call to Clay Roberts in Tallahassee seeking an extension to complete the count. A half-hour later, the request was turned down. An angry Burton then took a short break while LePore faxed to the capital a series of worksheets that supposedly had up-to-the-minute results. The board had decided to present the final tally the following morning, but did not in fact do so until the first week in December, at which time the net Gore pickup stood at 176 votes. For reasons not entirely clear, in both his brief and oral argument in the Florida Supreme Court contest case, Boies placed the Gore pickup in Palm

Beach County at 215 votes, a number the Justices tentatively adopted, but one having no basis in fact.

THE MILITARY VOTE

In the early 1980s, the federal government sued the state of Florida, claiming that the state's cumbersome procedures for filing absentee ballots effectively denied many overseas U.S. servicemen the right to vote. One problem was that a Florida election law requiring overseas absentee ballots to carry an APO, FPO, or foreign post mark invalidated the ballots of many servicemen who were victims of sloppy overseas posting services or who may have gotten their ballots back to the United States via a personal friend or courier or some other means of unofficial transportation.

In a consent decree entered in 1982, Florida pledged to address many of the problems in the U.S. complaint. Pursuant to that decree, the state adopted Rule IS-207 of the Florida Administrative Code which requires only that the ballot "be postmarked or (emphasis added) signed and dated no later than the date of the Federal election." The change was approved by the federal district court as part of the remedial action required by the consent decree.

Another problem—common to many states—involved a Florida requirement that requests for overseas absentee ballots be received by the state at least 30 days prior to the election. Mailed requests were frequently lost in transit or by state election officials, thus disenfranchising overseas voters. Congress addressed this situation in 1986 with the Uniformed and Overseas Citizens Absentee Voting Act (OCAVA). This permits overseas voters who have not received state ballots to cast a generic federal ballot. To protect against fraud, the overseas voter must sign an oath stating "that my application for a regular state absentee ballot was mailed intime to be received 30 days prior to this election." Clearly the oath is a substitute for physical proof of the effort to obtain the state ballot. Both the consent decree and the OCAVA had the force of law and, as anyone even reasonably schooled in the law would know, took precedence over any inconsistent Florida statutes or practices.

The Gore campaign, however, viewed the absentee military ballots received between Election Day and November 17 as a lethal threat. Bob Dole, the 1996 Republican candidate, who had lost Florida, nonetheless had received a hefty majority of the military absentee vote. Bush would likely top 60 percent at a time when he already enjoyed a 300-vote margin, which Gore was seeking to erase with selective recounts.

On November 15, Mark Herron, an attorney with the Gore campaign, circulated a five-page memorandum to Democratic lawyers across the state entitled "Overseas Absentee Ballot Review and Protest." The document described the grounds upon which absentee ballots could be challenged and included a "Protest of Overseas Absentee Ballot" form to make it easier for a challenger to file his protest.

Herron listed five particular areas in which Gore lawyers attending the county ballot counting should focus their attention. Item #1 instructed the lawyers to "determine that the voter affirmatively requested an overseas ballot," an instruction that resulted in challenges to federal write-in ballots supported only by the oath but with no receipt record in the county office.

Item #4 on Herron's list stated in part "with respect to those absentee ballots mailed by absolute qualified electors overseas, only those ballots mailed with an APO, FPO, or foreign postmark shall be considered valid." In the same paragraph, Herron acknowledged that his instructions were inconsistent with the Florida Administrative Code "which provides overseas absentee ballots may be accepted if 'postmarked or signed and dated no later than the date of the federal election.'"[19] In other words, from the face of his own memorandum, it would appear that Herron willfully instructed the Gore legal team to challenge overseas military absentee ballots on grounds he knew to be legally spurious.

Gore lawyers or observers were present in every county office in the state on November 17, seeking to keep as many military votes as possible from being counted. They were highly successful, particularly in counties controlled by Democrats. Overall, 356 overseas military ballots were disallowed because of postmark challenges and another 157 because there was no independent record of requests for absentee ballots having been received. Combined with other causes, a total of 788 military absentee ballots were rejected. Bush lawyers were also present in force. In counties carried by Bush, 29 percent of the overseas ballots were disallowed, but the figure was 60 percent in counties carried by Gore. In Duval County, the state's largest, which was carried by Bush, the canvassing board rejected 64 of 512 overseas absentee ballots. In Broward County, Gore's territory, the board rejected 304 of 396 ballots for a kill rate of 77 percent.[20]

Of those absentee ballots that were counted, Bush received 64 percent of the vote, picking up 1,380 votes to Gore's 750. This stretched Bush's lead over Gore to 930 votes pending the outcome of the selective recounts. And, for the moment, Gore had handed Bush a huge public relations victory. Dorrance Smith, a former ABC News executive producer and media director for President George H.W. Bush who had come to Florida at Baker's behest, immediately saw the potency of the issue and urged Austin to play it for all it was worth. Smith was soon talking up the story with the media gathered in Tallahassee. Before the Gore camp could blink, General Norman Schwarzkopf, the Persian Gulf war commander, was in Florida calling it "a very sad day in our country" when servicemen find that "because of some technicality out of their control they are denied the right to vote for the President of the United States, who will be their commander in chief."[21] Other Bush surrogates followed suit.

The Democrats at first tried to fire back publicly. Responding to the Republican onslaught, Bob Poe, Chairman of the state Democratic Party said, "I think that they wanted to get every military vote they could counted, regardless of the law."

In Washington, Senator Lieberman seemed to be more in touch with public opinion, telling NBC's Tim Russert, "If I was there, I would give the benefit of the doubt to ballots coming in from military personnel generally."[22] Florida county officials should "go back and take another look. Because again, Al Gore and I don't want to ever be part of anything that would put an extra burden on the military personnel abroad who want to vote." Lieberman's appeal took a bit of the fight out of Florida's Democrats on the issue. While some in the counties continued trying to block absentee ballots with any imperfection, the heavy hitters knew a lost cause when they saw one.

Attorney General Butterworth, possibly seeing his career aspirations flash before his eyes, publicly disassociated himself from the position of the Gore lawyers. In a letter to all county election supervisors and canvassing boards dated November 20, he wrote:

> No man or woman in military service to this nation should have his or her vote rejected solely due to the absence of a postmark, particularly when military officials have publicly stated that the postmarking of military mail is not always possible under sea or field conditions. Thus, canvassing boards should count overseas ballots, which are from qualified military electors and which bear no postmark if the ballot is signed and dated no later than the date of the election.[23]

Strategically, it was not obvious what the Bush team should do. Approaching the canvassing boards to reconsider their actions would generate some revisions, but, considering the recantations of top Democratic figures, the Bush lawyers were surprised to find a tough batch of Florida Democratic locals still fighting them tooth and nail. Further Bush could risk no legal move that would take the military ballots out of play for purposes of certification because, despite Herron's efforts, those ballots remained the margin of victory between the two candidates.

Fred Bartlit, the Bush lawyer handling the matter, next decided on a lawsuit in Leon County, but when that court publicly wondered whether it had jurisdiction, the Bush effort shifted to thirteen individual county courts. That wasn't much better, in part because Florida was then in its contest period in which only the loser could sue and everything took place in Leon County, home of the capital, Tallahassee. By then, the Bush lawyers in Tallahassee were beginning to ask each other some pointed questions about Bartlit's preparation. But the legal team finally found an appropriate forum for its complaint, the U.S. District Court for the Northern District of Florida in Pensacola. There, the Bush team asked for a declaratory judgment that certain specified grounds for invalidating overseas military ballots were illegal, and an injunction requiring the canvassing boards to reverse their rulings. That ruling would come in the form of a declaratory judgment and temporary restraining order issued by U.S. District Court Judge Lacey A. Collier on December 8 and 9, respectively. Judge Collier would order officials not to reject a federal write-in ballot that has been signed and dated "*solely* because the ballot or envelope does not have an APO, FPO, or foreign postmark;" or "*solely* because there is no record of an application for a state absentee ballot."[24]

Even before Judge Collier's ruling came down, canvassing officials in several counties that had voted for Bush had agreed to reverse enough of their overseas ballot exclusion decisions to beat the certification deadline, thus adding a net of 105 votes to the Bush victory margin. The Bush Tallahassee legal team expected the disrict court ruling to produce several hundred additional votes. But before Collier's Temporary Restraining Order could be implemented, the U.S. Supreme Court would halt all Florida electoral proceedings, putting Mr. Bush in the White House, but without the additional military votes.

On the evening of November 26, Secretary of State Katherine Harris announced at a staged yet somewhat fumbling ceremony that George W. Bush was the certified winner in Florida by 537 votes, the figure representing his 300-vote margin after the machine recounts, buttressed by his gain in the overseas absentee balloting, minus Gore's big gain in

Broward County. The "partial manual recount" submitted by Palm Beach County would not be counted. Having spent weeks at the epicenter of political controversy, Harris had concluded her essential business with a ministerial act. The contest phase of the Florida battle would barely involve her.

At the GOP headquarters in Tallahassee, the feeling was one of relief combined with resentment directed at Gore for continuing the struggle. Baker had some tough trial lawyers coming in from Houston and Chicago to handle the contest phase. He had also sent for Frank Donatelli, a Washington lawyer and veteran of the Reagan and Bush political operations, whose principal task would be to serve as liaison to the Florida legislature. Those familiar with Florida law were telling him that elections are very difficult to contest, but with the Florida Supreme Court certain to have another go at things, nothing was safe.

Baker and Austin agreed that it would be appropriate for the governor to address the country briefly after the certification. Stepping beyond his usual role of managing the Florida defense, Baker decided to have some of his Tallahassee people work on a draft.

The draft prepared by the Baker team reflected the combat attitude developed during nearly three weeks in the trenches. In prose as graceless as any statement from a "president-elect" could be, the Baker draft began with a curt "good evening" and continued:

> Tonight, three weeks after the election, the votes of Florida have been counted, confirmed and certified.
>
> This is now the fourth vote count that Secretary Cheney and I have won in that state. We had more votes than our opponents did on election night. We had more votes after the automatic recount. We had more votes in the election returns submitted on November 14. And now, once again, we have more votes—even after selective manual recounts, even under an extended deadline ordered by Florida's Supreme Court. We have won under the rules and laws passed by the Florida legislature. We have won under rules imposed by Florida's judges. We have won under procedures in place before the election, and under procedures created after the election.

The vice president has now exhausted every recount provision available to him. The result wasn't exactly a landslide. But by every count, and by any measure, we have carried the state of Florida.[25]

The draft went on to the mandatory call for finality of process: "At some point we must have an end. At some point, the counting must stop, and the votes must count. At some point, the law must prevail, and the lawyers must go home. And we have reached that point."

The draft had a half-life of instants. It quickly came back with brief comments from George W. Bush: "too arrogant, need better, softer way to say it, so pleased that secretary of state has confirmed, thank people of Florida."

Austin prepared a draft Bush liked better. It began: "The election was close, but tonight after a count, a recount, and yet another manual recount, Secretary Cheney and I are honored and humbled to have won the state of Florida, which gives us the needed electoral votes to win the election. We will therefore undertake the responsibility of preparing to serve as America's next president and vice president." Bush did add a modest call for Gore to close up shop. "This has been a hard-fought election, a healthy contest for American democracy. But now that the votes are counted, it is time for the votes to count."[26]

Baker himself addressed reporters on November 26. "Governor Bush and Secretary Cheney had more votes on Election Night," he barked. "They had more votes after the automatic recount. They had more votes in the election returns submitted by all of the counties on November 14."[27]

And so on. The speech may have been "too arrogant" to be delivered by the next president of the United States, but, with a few modifications it seemed just right for a tough old political strategist slugging it out in Florida but wishing he were off somewhere abbreviating the lives of pheasants.

CHAPTER 5

Vacating the Florida Court

On the afternoon of Friday, November 24, the U.S. Supreme Court surprised constitutional scholars throughout the country, including several on the Bush team, by granting the Bush petition for certiorari in the deadline extension case. The Bush petition had argued that the Florida Supreme Court had violated federal guidance (3 U.S.C. § 5) by changing the certification deadline, and that in doing so the state court had also violated Article 2 of the U.S. Constitution, which gives state legislatures the authority to determine how presidential electors are chosen. Tantalizingly, the Court had directed the parties to brief and argue an additional question: "What would be the consequences of this Court's finding that the decision of the Supreme Court of Florida does not comply with 3 U.S.C. § 5?"[1] The implication was that the statute that dealt with adjudication of challenges to state electors in the Congress was meant to explain how states could find a safe harbor against challenges rather than providing an avenue for judicial review.

The Bush petition had also raised with the Court the issue of whether the combination of selective recounts and seemingly random counting rules violated the First and Fourteenth Amendments, but the Supreme Court denied certiorari on that series of issues. Weeks later, liberal critics would suggest that the partisan court had mouse-trapped Gore by postponing consideration of the issue until there was no time to remedy the problem. But with the matter still before the Eleventh Circuit and Florida still having the opportunity to cure the problem during its contest period, a compelling case can be made that the issue was simply not ripe for adjudication.

Olson, Carvin, and the other appellate lawyers were now predicting victory before the U.S. Supreme Court. They believed that even the four needed votes to grant certiorari wouldn't have been there had an incipient majority for reversal not been there. But coming as it did after Miami-Dade County had abandoned its recount and Palm Beach, facing its own deadline crunch, had adopted standards minimizing the Gore pickup, the victory at the Court presented as many complications as potential benefits. Certification of the Bush Florida victory was expected Sunday evening. How could a win in the U.S. Supreme Court help? What might it do to options of the state legislature, which had retained counsel and was preparing to file an amicus brief? Further, Gore had already announced plans to contest the election following certification, thus assuring a critical role for the Florida courts. What impact could a U.S. Supreme Court decision have there? As Baker, Ginsberg, Zoellick, Terwilliger, Bolten, and others discussed the event, some in the room began to argue that the Supreme Court case should be dropped. Bush could continue to press his Due Process and Equal Protection claims with the federal courts, but this case now risked too much for too little. Zoellick in particular argued that nothing the Florida Supreme Court could do would enable Gore to overtake a Bush lead of 537 votes, soon to be augmented by additional military absentee ballots.

Baker disagreed. He wanted a win over the Florida courts in the Supreme Court of the United States. But when Zoellick pleaded that the issue should be presented to Bush in the form of a decision memo, Baker agreed. Entitled "Background on Post-Recount Options," the paper emphasized that dropping the case should only be considered if Bush won certification Sunday night, and that "the window to drop the case is *only* immediately after certification of the recount results (Sunday evening or Monday morning). The paper continued:

Reasons for dropping the case

• Our prospects for winning the case, while better than even, are highly uncertain. If we lose the case after eking out a narrow win in the vote count, Gore will be seen as scoring a big victory, which he will use to lend momentum and legitimacy to his contest challenges in Florida courts.

• If we lose the case, the ruling could backfire on us by posing major political and/or legal impediments to any action by the Florida legislature to overturn Florida court decisions for Gore in the contest proceedings.

• Dropping the case would remove a Gore excuse for continuing to litigate and would reinforce a Bush call to rely on the numerous counts of the voting results rather than litigation.

Reasons for continuing the case

• A Supreme Court win might remove the basis for Gore's election contest. At a minimum, it would create enormous public pressure for Gore to drop his contest.

• It would look bad to drop the case now. Furthermore, as long as the case is pending, the Florida Supreme Court is likely to be more careful in ruling on contest proceedings.

• It makes more sense to maintain the Supreme Court route if we are not absolutely determined to use the legislative route.

• Our supporters in the Florida Legislature would probably not look kindly on our dropping the case.

In terms of Sunday night options, the memo listed dropping the Supreme Court case and all other litigation and urging

Gore to do the same, continuing the case and all other litigation, and:

> "Offer to drop the Supreme Court case and all litigation if Gore drops all litigation. Emphasizes that it's time to draw a line under all the counts and recounts. 'Offer' loses nothing, but public will recognize that it's really a rhetorical tactic, because if Gore accepts he loses."[2]

Soon after receiving the memo, Bush replied, choosing to stay with the case. "Bush and Cheney wanted legitimacy," Zoellick later suggested. "They never felt they could get it from the legislature. So they stayed with the Court."

By specifically asking for guidance on 3 U.S.C. § 5, the Court had confronted Olson, Carvin, and others who worked on the brief with the distinct possibility of having the court declare the issue non-justiciable. On its face, it seemed to offer guidance to the states and direction to the Congress but nothing further. Yet the Bush brief argued that if the Court found the Florida Supreme Court had changed the law either by using its equitable powers to organize a new certification schedule or by allowing the introduction of new counting standards, it should vacate the Florida decision. "The resulting consequences are twofold. First, the executive officials in Florida would be able to discharge all of their duties imposed by federal law in place on Election Day. Second, Congress would be able to give conclusive effect to the official certification of the Elections Canvassing Commission regarding the appointment of Florida's electors made pursuant to the carefully crafted scheme put in place before the election to apply equally to all voters and candidates."[3] A nice try, certainly, but not even faintly responsive to the question the court had asked. The question Olson answered was, what effect would vacating the Florida decision have? What the U.S. Supreme Court wanted to know was, where from the language of the code do we get the power to vacate in the first place?

Here Olson missed an opportunity to drive home what should have been the central Bush theme: the distinction between the legislature changing the law after the election, and the court doing so. When the legislature flaunts 3 U.S.C. § 5, it loses for its state the "safe harbor," which protects the electoral delegation of the state from challenge. But when a court changes the law, it is violating Article 2 of the U.S. Constitution, which assigns the power to determine election procedures to the various state legislatures. That means its actions are reviewable and reversible by the U.S. Supreme Court, while a legislative action that, say, extends a recount deadline, would not be.

Representing Gore in the Supreme Court was Laurence Tribe, the gifted Harvard constitutional scholar whose credibility had been compromised only marginally by his rush to endorse the butterfly ballot challenge. Reduced to basics, his brief maintained that rather than changing laws helter-skelter, the Florida Supreme Court had employed four time-tested techniques of statutory construction: where laws conflict, the more specific rule controls the less specific one; in cases of conflict, the more recent law controls the more distant one; statutes should be interpreted so as to avoid making any particular provision meaningless or absurd; and, the court will try to interpret a series of laws as a coherent whole. Every one of its actions could be explained by one or more of the traditional approaches to the law, Tribe maintained.

Unable to join the lawsuit as a party because it was not in session and thus could not get the authority to do so, both houses of the legislature joined in an amicus brief authored by former Solicitor General Charles Fried and Einer Elhague, both of Harvard Law School. Their central argument was that the entire issue was non-justiciable in that the power to determine presidential electoral college selection rested with the state legislature, and hence the right to judge whether the Florida Supreme Court had ordered procedures compatible with its direction rested first with the legislature and finally with the Congress, which had to approve elector slates sent by the states.

As he read the legislature's brief, Frank Donatelli realized that he had to navigate a complex course to convert the great theoretical advantage of an overwhelmingly Republican institution into a practical one. Here, for example, was a clear disparity of interest. The Bush team was asking the Supreme Court to intervene and vacate a decision by the Florida Supreme Court. At the same time, the legislature was saying that neither court had any business in the case, that interpreting the law should be up to the state legislature with the final imprimatur applied by the United States Congress. Maybe in theory that case is strong, but in practice it assumed that Bush would want to be declared president by the Florida legislature, perhaps after losing one of the recount battles. And it assumed that a scenario like that could play nationally.

Nor was this the only difference of emphasis. Bush was looking for a quick legislative finding that by tampering with the recount deadlines and permitting wildly divergent counting standards, the Florida Supreme Court had changed the rules of the election after the election. The legislature, on the other hand, viewed the potential failure to achieve a safe harbor as its trigger for selecting the electoral college slate, something which would not be known with certainty until December 12.

The Bush lawyers examined Florida's history and found that back in the 1872 Hayes-Tilden contest the legislature had designated its electors for Hayes by passing a bill. The Bush team saw no constitutional precedent to support a joint resolution. However, House Speaker Tom Feeney and his advisor, a former Oklahoma state legislator named Don Rubottom, didn't want to consider legislation. First, they said it would take too long. Second, a bill would require the governor's signature, something they felt undermined the constitutional sanctity of their plenary power.

Then too there was the question of direct versus contingent appointment of the elector slate. Donatelli and the Bush lawyers liked the idea of contingent appointment because the legislature could act immediately to name a Bush slate contingent on matters not being resolved by December 12. Legislative leaders, on the other hand, felt they could step in under Florida law only if the dispute had not been finally resolved by the deadline. That meant there would be no safe harbor and even a Bush legislative victory could be challenged in the Congress. In formulating the question of whether or not to stay with the Supreme Court case, Bob Zoellick had made the point that the legislature offered greater certainty but the Supreme Court of the United States offered greater legitimacy. To Donatelli, the closest thing to a certainty was that December 12 was going to arrive without anyone knowing with certainty who the next president would be.

In the end, neither side walked away from the December 1 U.S. Supreme Court argument with very much confidence. The justices did everything but tweak the noses and cuff the ears of the arguing counsel like so many errant schoolboys. Olson never seemed to clear the hurdle of Article 3 U.S.C. § 5 being a matter dealing with the states, allowing the Congress no judicial function. Justice Scalia memorably compared the statute to a law granting federal funds to states that maintain a 55-mph speed limit. If the state court interprets state law as permitting a 65-mph speed, the state simply does without the money; it does not invite federal court intervention.

Nor did Olson appear to satisfy the court on what practical difference it would make if the Justices found an Article 5 problem with the state supreme court ruling, because that section was there principally to guide the Congress. He seemed to do better when the question turned to whether the Florida Court had changed the law, arguing to Justice Kennedy at one point, "But what it did was supplant a set of rules enacted before the election to govern the election for a set of rules made up after the election."[4] Though temperate and professional in explaining his problems with the decision below, Olson may also have paid a price with one justice for

Baker's indelicate reaction to the Florida decision. At one point Justice Ginsburg remarked, "I do not know of any case where we have impugned a state supreme court the way you are doing in this case. I mean, in case after case, we have said we owe the highest respect to what the state supreme court says is the state's law."[5] The Justice's vex could better have been directed at the Florida court whose unrestrained activism had produced the legal train wreck.

Joe Klock, representing Katherine Harris, tried to persuade the Court that, even in the wake of Bush' certification, their decision could be of critical importance to the outcome of the election. "Your Honor," said Klock, "if the law is returned to the point it was on November 7, there is no right to a manual recount to correct voter error, and that will end the litigation that currently exists in the state of Florida."[6] Given the low bar the Florida Justices would erect for initiating a recount during the contest period, Klock's prognosis was probably optimistic.

The court pursued the point with Paul Hancock, who was representing the state attorney general as he had in the Florida court. He was asked if "you know of any other elections in Florida in which recounts were conducted, manual recounts, because of an allegation that some voters did not punch the cards the way they should have through their fault?

Hancock: No, Justice—
Question: Did that ever happen—
Hancock: No, I'm not aware of it ever happening before . . .[7]

The admission would prove harmless to the case at bar. But less than two weeks later it would be one of a number of factors noted by the majority as reflecting the overreaching of the Florida justices.

Tribe had one serious problem and one fatal problem. The serious problem was that the Florida court, despite its lip service to statutory construction, had in fact changed the law, particularly in revising the recount deadline. At one point an exasperated Justice Kennedy fumed, "And if the legislature had jumped into the breach and said this same thing, would that bc a new statute or new enactment under 5 U.S.C.?"[8] Tribe had no credible answer.

Tribe's fatal problem was that the state supreme court had held that the Florida constitution venerating the right to vote made it impossible for the secretary of state to impose the rigid statutory deadline on manual recounts. That ran counter to the U.S. Supreme Court's 1892 ruling in *McPherson v. Blacker*, which held that federal law granted plenary power to state legislatures to determine the selection of presidential electors, a power that could not be constrained even by the state constitution. When Tribe suggested that the state court had merely used the Florida constitution as a means of interpreting how the legislature intended the deadline law to work, Justice Scalia challenged Tribe to "give me one sentence in the opinion that supports . . . the proposition that the Florida Supreme Court was using the constitutional right to vote provisions as an interpretive tool to determine what the statute meant. I can't find a single sentence for that."[9]

Tribe did his best, suggesting that the structure of the opinion suggested the court engaged first in ordinary games of statutory construction before invoking the state constitution to support an interpretation already reached. But it was no use. Even Justice Ginsburg was ready to give some ground, saying, "I suppose there would be a possibility for this court to remand for clarification."[10]

That road could at least preserve the appearance of unity on a Court already divided on the question of deference to the naked activism of the Florida tribunal. The price of unity was at this point cheap because George W. Bush had already achieved certification and two of the three remaining recount counties had failed to meet even the extended deadline. Further, it was not clear what impact an alternative course would have. Reversing the Florida court by, for example, holding the seven-day period sacrosanct would temporarily deprive Gore of the 567 votes he had picked up in Broward County, but with the contest period now in full swing, the state court could issue a ruling putting those votes back in his column and authorizing recounts elsewhere. Holding for Gore, on the other hand, would not change the totals but would send a nod of approval in the direction of the Florida court just as the critical contest issues were ripening.

On December 4, hours before Circuit Court Judge Sanders Sauls would strike down the Gore contest challenge unequivocally, the U.S. Supreme Court issued a unanimous per curium ruling vacating the Florida Supreme Court decision, finding "considerable uncertainty as to the precise grounds for the decision." The court said it was "unclear as to the extent to which the Florida Supreme Court saw the Florida Constitution as circumscribing the legislature's authority." It was also "unclear as to the consideration the Florida Supreme Court accorded to 3 U.S.C. § 5." Although declining to resolve the federal questions pending clarification from the court below, the U.S. Supreme Court warned the Florida Supreme Court that "a legislative wish to take advantage of the 'safe harbor' would counsel against any construction of the Election Code that Congress might deem to be a change in the law."[11]

This unanimous warning regarding the sanctity of the December 12 date would prove critical one week later when a bare majority of justices—after finding that Florida's procedures violated Equal Protection and Due Process—held that there was no reason to permit the state Supreme Court to attempt to refine those procedures as they could not possibly meet the December 12 deadline.

The Florida Supreme Court asked both sides to file briefs by the following day on how the U.S. Supreme Court remand should affect the Court's decision. The ambitious deadline seemed to indicate that the Court would quickly take advantage of the road map provided by the U.S. Supreme Court and announce a decision consistent both with its earlier result and with what it hoped the U.S. court would accept. For inexplicable reasons, that never happened. To the obvious annoyance of at least one U.S. justice, Florida would not send a revised opinion to the U.S. Supreme Court until its more definitive ruling in the contest case had been argued. For that indiscretion, Justice Sandra Day O'Connor would deliver a rebuke from the bench during oral argument on the case that would decide the presidency.

In Tallahassee, the Bush team had expected victory in the U.S. Supreme Court and their irritation at gaining something less was compounded as they watched David Boies spinning the press with suggestions that the decision changed nothing and merely required clarification that the state could easily provide. That was surely not true, the lawyers felt. The Supreme Court had not merely remanded the Florida decision, which it clearly could have done, but vacated it as well. In the short run, this meant that anything Gore might have gained from Broward, Miami-Dade, or Palm Beach was wiped from the slate. And to get those numbers back, the Florida Supreme Court would have to persuade five Justices in Washington that it had acted within the law.

Terwilliger felt the decision had changed the landscape. "What the Supreme Court did was to put a very hot round close to the bow of the Florida Supreme Court," he said. They will have to walk carefully in the contest case if that goes our way, he thought. This will not again be the feisty group that two weeks ago was busy rewriting the Florida election law. Later Baker would tell the press, "We are gratified by the U.S. Supreme Court decision today. Let me be clear. This decision was *unanimous*. This decision *vacated* the Florida Supreme Court ruling. And it did so on the reservations we've expressed about this decision in the past."

That may have been true, but the decision was by no means conclusive. Vacated or not, the Florida Supreme Court was essentially invited to do a little patchwork here and there and return something that could be accepted upon review. Perhaps that was a good indication of where the Justices stood at this moment. Still, neither in brief nor in argument had Olson answered the Supreme Court's basic question in a way that would have framed the issue perfectly for the Bush side. Yes, it makes a difference for the Court to find that the Florida Justices, in changing the dates of the protest period, had violated 3 U.S.C. § 5. And the difference is critical. Had the legislature made such a change, the only consequence would have been to deny the state the benefit of the statutory "safe harbor" provided by Congress. But where the change is made by the state judiciary, that violates Article 2 of the Constitution as well, because that article reposes plenary power for fashioning presidential election procedures to the various state legislatures. And the only cure for the violation is to make Florida adhere to the original deadlines. That would not only have restored the Bush margins to the pre-recount period, but it would likely have preempted recounts during the contest period because Gore would have had no basis on which to challenge the certified returns.

There was little time, however, to dissect the Supreme Court decision or the legal arguments that had influenced it. By early afternoon, word had come from the circuit court that Judge Sauls was ready to deliver his decision.

CHAPTER **6**

Surviving a Scare

Daryl Bristow, the white-maned, elegant trial lawyer from the Baker & Botts firm in Houston, was well into preparation for his role in the defense against Gore's contest suit when he received a call from his senior Houston partner. It was Wednesday, November 29.

"Daryl," said Baker, "I'm going to ask you to do something with no upside. If you win, no one will give you credit because it's a case that's too easy to win. If you lose, you'll always be known as the guy who blew the big one."

Bristow knew that Baker was referring to the lawsuits filed by Gore supporters in Seminole and Martin counties. They were asking the courts to throw out more than 15,000 absentee ballots because Republican officials had been permitted to correct voter identification numbers incorrectly printed or left out altogether on request forms for the ballots.[1] Ginsberg's legal team had conducted a cursory review of the claims and determined them to be lacking in merit if not altogether frivolous, so the cases had plunked along off the radar screen in the two counties during the protest phase of the Florida battle. But now that the two sides had moved into the contest period, the cases, like all others, had been transferred to Leon County, where they were generating national media coverage.

Baker explained the concerns that had led him to ask Bristow to handle the matter. First, the absentee ballots in the two counties had provided Bush with a margin of more than 7,000 votes. Should he lose either case, Bush's battle for the presidency would be lost. Second, the cases involved textbook examples of state law, lacking the federal hook, for example, of Equal Protection or Due Process. Were Bush to lose in the Florida courts he would have a much tougher time getting U.S. Supreme Court attention than he might in lawsuits challenging selective manual recounts or changes in the certification deadline. Finally, the Seminole County case had been assigned to Circuit Court Judge Nikki Ann Clark—black, female, Democrat—a one-person demographic nightmare, and a former aide to Governor Lawton Chiles. Moreover, Judge Clark had recently been passed over by Governor Jeb Bush for appointment to the District Court of Appeals, a move which Florida sources said had left her deeply hurt. Should she rule on behalf of the plaintiffs, the best that could happen would be an appeal to the Florida Supreme Court and its outcome-oriented band of judicial ad-libbers. And even that shot at relief was not considered a sure thing because a narrow reading of state contest laws could lead a jurist to conclude that the legislature had vested sole jurisdiction in the circuit courts, permitting no appellate review.

By the time the two men had concluded their discussion, Bristow was making plans to fly to Orlando to begin taking depositions in the case. In doing so, he was stepping into a case from which Gore and his immediate political family had, for purely tactical reasons, chosen to distance themselves, but one in which their behind-the-scenes role was substantial. The importance of the case to Gore would be emphasized when, during the first week of December, the vice president himself sought to summarize it for reporters in a way that distorted the record beyond recognition.

What happened in Seminole and Martin counties was the result of a clerical error by a veteran Dallas direct mail firm, James Foster and Associates, hired by Florida Republicans to prepare absentee ballot requests for GOP voters residing abroad. A Florida statute that provides that such forms must include the name and address of the voter and the last four digits of the voter's social security number, had been amended in 1998 to require as well the number on the voter's registration card, thereby providing election officials with an additional means of determining that those requesting absentee ballots were in fact eligible to vote. The request forms mailed out by the Democratic Party included either a space where the person making the request could provide his or her voter registration identification number, or in some cases, the proper number itself. In contrast, the forms distributed by the Foster firm did not include a number or space for one, or any indication that such a number need be furnished.

Barely mentioned by the media was the fact that the Republican oversight was not limited to Seminole and Martin counties. Others too had been touched by the GOP negligence, but when the problem surfaced elsewhere, county election officials, recognizing that they had adequate means of identifying the voters without the identification numbers, treated the problem as de minimus and mailed off the requested ballots. Only the supervisor of elections in Seminole County, Sandra Goard, and her counterpart in Martin County, Stewart Hershey, set the imperfect forms aside, refusing to process them.

Republican Party officials contacted Goard requesting permission to send representatives to her office to correct or complete the ballot request forms. She agreed. Michael Leach, the north Florida regional director for the GOP, assisted occasionally by one or two others, corrected the request forms. Commissioner Goard then mailed the absentee ballots overseas, and thousands of voters abroad cast ballots before the November 7 deadline. Interestingly, the Democratic ballot request forms from Seminole County were returned not to Goard directly but to House Victory 2000, the nerve center of the state's Democratic operation, where party workers prepared the envelopes for delivery to the election commissioner's office. In terms of the opportunity for tampering, there was thus no functional difference between the parties.

An identical process took place in Martin County save the fact that there, county officials permitted Republican workers to remove the ballot application forms from the county office, returning them after they had been corrected.

Striking about the process was its openness. The GOP problem in Seminole County was discussed in local radio news reports and Leach, armed with his personal laptop computer, made the corrections in the county office during regular working hours. Local Democratic Party officials were aware of the activity but offered no protest. Bob Poe, the state Democratic chairman, did complain to Goard in October, but was unable to persuade her that the activity was inappropriate. Only after the election did Harry Jacobs, a flamboyant Seminole County Democrat and lawyer, initiate legal action.

The Bush lawyers who perused the case concluded immediately that it was without merit. Two leading Florida Supreme Court decisions seemed dispositive of the issue. In *Boardman v. Esteva*,[2] the court declined to exclude more than 1300 absentee ballots in a race for a court of appeals judgeship despite a showing of minor irregularities, including failure to state the reason for voting absentee and omitting the addresses of attesting witnesses. The court held that because the will of the voters was the primary consideration, substantial compliance with election laws was enough: "It is the policy of the law to prevent the disenfranchisement of electors who have cast their ballots in good faith, and while the technical requirements set for the absentee law are mandatory, yet in meeting these requirements laws are construed so that a substantial compliance therewith is all that is required."

Boardman contained other language that was of central importance to the Seminole and Martin cases. Statutes often contain provisions that serve to guide executive agencies but that, if ignored, do not invalidate their actions. The 1975 court held that unless the statute specifically provides that the failure to obey a particular provision invalidates the vote, "the statute should be treated as directory, not mandatory, provided such irregularity is not calculated to affect the integrity of the ballot or election." Thus, for example, an election board cannot under Florida law count the ballot of an absentee voter who fails to include on his ballot the date he voted. That requirement is *mandatory*. But an application may be sent to a voter who leaves his voter identification number off the request form because that provision is *directory*.

The disinclination of the courts to disturb the expressed will of voters in the absence of fraud was underlined in the more recent case, *Beckstrom v. Volusia County*. The case involved an election for sheriff in which absentee ballots that did not register a vote on their first feed through an optical scanner were manually marked by election officials with a felt tip pen and rescreened. Had the officials followed previously instituted guidelines they would have made copies of the undercounted ballots and marked the copy for scanning while preserving the original ballot in a designated envelope. Here the action of election officials was both grossly negligent and rife with opportunities for fraud. However, no fraud was evident. Indeed, the affected ballots included a higher percentage of undervotes and a lower percentage of overvotes than ballots not subject to manual intervention. Had the canvassing board been filling in blank ballots, there would have been fewer undervotes. Had it been defiling ballots by adding names, there would have been more overvotes.

"We simply conclude that the court should not frustrate the will of the voters if the failure to perform official duties is unintentional wrongdoing and the will of the voters can be determined," held the court.[3]

Both *Boardman* and *Beckstrom* were right on point. The difference between a "mandatory" and "directory" provision of the law was critical, and here it favored the Bush absentee voters. The Bush lawyers simply saw nothing to fear in Seminole and Martin counties. The law was on their side, unequivocally.

For Gore, who had adopted the "count every vote" mantra early during the selective recount battle, Seminole and Martin counties provided a delicate political problem. Potentially they represented victory in the election in one luscious gobble. But embracing the effort by adding it to the contest lawsuit would be viewed by the press and blasted by Republicans as a cynical desperation move, particularly coming on the heels of the much-criticized effort to block the counting of military absentee ballots.

So the Gore team decided to play it both ways, publicly distancing the vice president from the case but effectively taking over the litigation by providing counsel to the Seminole plaintiff and orchestrating a public relations campaign, on one occasion involving Gore himself, that would present an egregiously false picture of what had actually transpired. One of Gore's closest allies in the labor movement, Jack Dempsey, the general counsel of the American Federation of State, County, and Municipal Employees, helped coordinate the efforts in both Seminole and Martin counties. Meanwhile, Joe Sandler, chief counsel to the DNC, recruited Gerald Richman, a leading Palm Beach lawyer, as Jacobs's attorney.

The Gore involvement didn't stop there. Jacobs acknowledged in a pretrial deposition that he had met with Gore's lawyer, Mitchell Berger. The meeting was also attended by Richman. Reporting on the conversation, the *Washington Post* quoted Berger telling Richman, "We're England, and you're the United States. We're beleaguered here, and you're the one that has the chance to come through."[4]

Days after that meeting, Richman received a call from Steven Kirsch, a Silicon Valley billionaire and generous Gore contributor, who promptly volunteered $150,000 to finance the Seminole County case and followed that up with a similar donation to the Martin County plaintiffs. The money permitted the Gore surrogates to retain a public relations specialist who began what proved to be a successful effort to interest the national media in the two cases. Suddenly stories began to appear suggesting that the cases not only involved tampering with absentee ballot applications, but also wildly disparate treatment of similar Republican and Democratic situations in Seminole County, and conduct by election officials that was punishable as a felony under Florida law.

Gore himself got into the act on December 5. Asked by the Washington press about the Seminole and Martin county cases, the vice president replied as follows:

> Well, there were more than enough votes to make the differenc, that were apparently thrown into . . . the applications for ballots were thrown into the trash can by the supervisor of elections there, apparently, even though they were missing the same number that the Republican Party workers were allowed to come in and fix the other applications with. So I don't want to speculate on what the remedy might be; I'm not a party to that case or the Martin County case. But more than enough votes were potentially taken away from Democrats, because they were not given the same access that Republicans were. Remember, according to what's come out in that case; again, I'm not a party to it, but I've read about it.

Gore continued:

> Apparently the Democratic Party chair was denied the opportunity to even look at the list of applications, whereas the Republican Party workers were allowed to roam around unsupervised inside the office and bring their computers in and fix all of the valid applications for one side even as the Democrats were denied an opportunity to come in, denied a chance to even look at the applications and those applications were thrown out. Now, that doesn't seem fair to me.[5]

As the facts acknowledged by both sides would soon show, contrary to Gore's account there had been no Democratic forms thrown away in the wastebasket or anywhere else and no discrimination against the Democratic Party of any kind. The missing voter identification numbers were exclusively a Republican problem. And as such there was no need to permit any special Democratic access because no Democratic ballot applications were in danger of being disallowed.

Bristow saw the core of his case as sound but fretted about the fringes. Barry Richard was telling him he could expect fair treatment from Judge Clark, but other Florida veterans were warning that she was a judicial time bomb waiting to explode. Bristow felt he could take no chances and moved first to consolidate the two cases under Judge Terry Lewis, who had ruled for Katherine Harris on the recount extension. Then he moved for Judge Clark to recuse herself due to her strong anti-Bush feelings arising from the Florida governor's failure to promote her. Both motions were lost.

"That was a mistake," Bristow later said. "After fifteen minutes in her courtroom, I knew we would get a fair decision. Judge Clark takes control. She inspires confidence."

In Bristow's written pleadings, the Bush lawyers took the further precaution of trying to inject federal issues into the case. The hope was to preserve a hook for the federal courts just in case things went awry in Florida. Citing a civil rights-era provision of the federal code that forbids anyone acting under color of law to "deny the right of any individual to vote in any election because of an error or omission on any record or paper relating to any application, registration, or other act requisite to voting, if such error or omission is not material in determining whether such individual is qualified under state law to vote in such election."[6]

Powerful stuff, to be sure. But Bristow knew the problem was that if the Florida courts interpreted the violation as *material* to voter qualification, the federal courts would be hard-pressed to overrule that conclusion.

Both Bristow and others were impressed when, early in the trial, Judge Clark went matter-of-factly about her business, ignoring the glaring presence of the Reverend Jesse Jackson in her courtroom. As Jackson lacked a documented intellectual fascination with the arcane vicissitudes of Florida election law, Bristow could only assume that Jackson's presence was intended to fortify, or perhaps intimidate, Judge Clark into delivering a decision favorable to the candidate who had won 93 percent of the votes cast by African-Americans nationwide.

Bristow's other problem involved potential witnesses. Sandra Goard was a career public servant—quiet, fragile, and frightened. The two Republican Party officials who had actually corrected the ballots in each county, Michael Leach and Todd Schnitt, were potential problems. Leach was right-wing even by the standards of conservative Florida Republicans and maintained a political Web site that, if it came into play, could expose the Bush campaign to ridicule. Schnitt, on the other hand, seemed unduly nervous about the proceedings and there was no way to predict how he would act on the stand.

So Bristow decided to take advantage of everyone's desire to save time, particularly with both trials scheduled to take place on a rotating basis in the same Tallahassee courtroom. He had his team draft a lengthy stipulation, admitting to 95 percent of the facts the other side was prepared to place on the record through its own witnesses and cross-examination. To his delight, Richman agreed. Leach never took the stand in either case because few facts were in dispute. Goard too, a potentially nervous witness who had exercised zero supervision over her Republican visitors, was spared from having to testify. And Schnitt's testimony did minimal damage in the Martin County case even though he froze when plaintiff's counsel asked him whether he realized that by tampering with the absentee ballot applications he had committed a "third-degree felony."

Both Judges Clark and Lewis released their decisions just after 2:30 P.M. on December 8 as the nation awaited what many expected to be the definitive resolution of the 2000 election by the Florida Supreme Court. The two judges found for Bush on all material issues. Indeed, Judge Lewis noted that because the provision of a voter identification number was directory rather than mandatory, election officials could have mailed the ballots to the absentee voters without requiring any fix. "The failure to comply with the statutory procedure was not intentional wrongdoing, but rather was the result of an erroneous understanding of the statutory requirements. There is also no basis in the evidence to conclude that the irregularities affected the vote."

Nor did either jurist find any basis for suggestions that Democrats had been treated differently than Republicans in the two counties. The Democrats had simply never had the voter identification number problem, so there had been no need for them to participate in the cure. As Judge Clark concluded, "For all the foregoing reasons, the court finds that the certified election in Seminole County was the result of the fair expression of the will of the people of Seminole County."[7] Justice Lewis also concluded that despite the minor irregularities, "the sanctity of the ballot and the integrity of the election were not affected."[8]

Four days later, the Florida Supreme Court unanimously affirmed both decisions. By then, of course, Seminole and Martin Counties were again off the radar, about as far off as two counties can get.

CHAPTER 7

Fighting the Contest

David Boies did not wait for Katherine Harris to perform the ministerial act of certification Sunday evening, November 26, before sharing with the press his strategy for seeking to have the certification thrown out in a lawsuit to be filed in the circuit court for Leon County the following day. The 168 votes that Gore had picked up in the heavily Democratic precincts of Miami-Dade County during the aborted recount should remain with the vice president, because they were clearly legal votes, according to Boies. In addition, Boies said, "There are approximately 10,000 ballots [in Miami-Dade] that have never been counted once for the presidential election, and it is those so-called undervote ballots that we will be contesting."[1]

Boies also affirmed plans to include "the inexplicable actions in Nassau County" in the lawsuit. Due to human error, 218 votes tabulated on election night were not fed into computers during the automatic recount, resulting in a net loss of 52 votes for George W. Bush. Thanks to the extended certification deadline, Nassau officials had time to confer with the secretary of state, who advised the county simply to go back to the first, more accurate count. Understandably, the Gore team preferred the second, though inaccurate one.

Boies further suggested that Nassau officials had suddenly "replaced one member of its canvassing board with another individual, who appears to be ineligible under Florida law."[2] The "new" board then went back to the initial total. Instead of seeking a manual recount—the obvious way to challenge the canvassing board's final count—Boies said he would simply ask the circuit court to strike down its revised computation and subtract 52 votes from the Bush totals.

Boies also reminded reporters that Gore had problems with the Palm Beach counting techniques, not to mention Ms. Harris's refusal to include recounted votes that had not met the 5 P.M. deadline imposed by the state supreme court.

And what about the December 12 deadline that had, during weeks of litigation, become the date before which all disputes, including appeals, must be resolved? That deadline was only 16 days away when Boies filed this contest motion. Could the thousands of ballots be counted and all judicial proceedings resolved within this time?

Boies offered one shortcut to help meet the date: "What we obviously would hope is that that process of reviewing ballots would start very promptly, hopefully as early as Tuesday. It'll probably take until Tuesday to get the ballots from Dade County and from Palm Beach County."[3]

From his office at the state Republican headquarters, Phil Beck watched Boies go through his routine like a commentator watching a champion figure skater work through his mandatory program. Beck, along with his partner, Fred Bartlit, and the bearish, supercompetitive Irv Terrell of Houston, would take the lead in interrogating and cross-examining witnesses for Bush. Each was regarded by colleagues—and by himself—as a fair match for David Boies. By contrast, Dexter Douglas, Mitchell Berger, Steven Zack, Kendal Coffey, and other Gore lawyers appeared as satellites bearing only the reflected luster of Boies, their star. Richard would deliver the opening and closing arguments for the Bush team. Beck had litigated against Boies once before, as the attorney for General Motors in its battle against H. Ross Perot, whom Boies represented. He thought of Boies as an excellent lawyer, a nice guy, friendly, civil, cooperative, and professional, but far from invincible.

Yes, Boies was good, smooth, and talented. But here in Florida, he had also become predictable, his repertoire well known. And with every press conference, every appearance on Larry King Live, he and his program became even better known. Obviously, the central issues in the litigation were as Boies had stated: the Palm Beach counting techniques, the deadline imposed by the supreme court, and the truncated Miami-Dade recount. The new disclosure was that Boies was going to try to get the counting going before prevailing on a single legal point in the circuit court. The Bush team would be ready for that.

Beck, whose assignment would be to handle the critical cross-examination of the Gore witnesses, also had a mental file on two he thought would be central to the Gore case. Kimball Brace, a New York-based election and redistricting consultant, and Nicholas Hengartner, a Yale statistics professor, had both filed affidavits before Judge Labarga in Palm Beach. Brace had offered an explanation as to how the deterioration of rubber coupled with the buildup of chads in the Votomatic machines can allegedly make it difficult to punch through the ballot. Hengartner projected a Gore pickup sufficient to win Florida if the complete results from Palm Beach County were included, the 157 net Miami-Dade Gore votes from the aborted recount were added, and the 9,000 remaining undervotes were examined. Beck thought neither witness impressive, and would be astonished when, at trial, they proved to be the only two Boies would put on the stand.

The case had been assigned to Judge Sanders Sauls, a burly, courtly man with a taste for homily and a touch of temper. In an earlier era, Sauls might well have been described as a "Yaller-Dog" Democrat, one more likely to cast a vote for a yellow dog than a Republican. But Strom Thurmond, Barry Goldwater, and Ronald Reagan had turned many a "Yaller-Dog" Democrat into a Republican, and many of those, like Sauls, who for personal reasons remained within the Democratic Party, had time and again shown themselves more comfortable with Republican candidates at the national level than their own party's candidates. Sauls, in short, was about as good a selection to preside over the contest trial as the Bush team could have hoped for, and as tough as the Gore camp could have feared.

As Boies had indicated, Gore filed his suit November 27, attacking the votes recorded in Palm Beach, Miami-Dade, and Nassau Counties and requesting the advertised relief. It was the first time the certified results of any presidential election had been challenged in the courts and the first contest ever of a statewide Florida race. The section of the Florida code under which the action was brought was 102.168. The relevant grounds for contesting an election under that section include "receipt of a number of illegal votes or rejection of a number of legal votes sufficient to change or place in doubt the result of the election." These grounds stated in the Florida code gave rise to two questions that would dominate the trial before Judge Sauls as well as the argument before the state supreme court.

First, what standard of evidence must a plaintiff meet to "place in doubt the result of the election"? Boise would claim that if the results of the recommended recount could be projected as breaking in the same ratio as the partial recount, the outcome of the contest could be changed and Gore would have satisfied the statute, thus earning the judicial recount. The Bush team would argue that Gore must establish by a preponderance of the evidence a reasonable probability that the results would be different.

Second, does the circuit court assess the evidence de novo, in essence becoming an automatic recount service for Gore, or must the vice president establish that the canvassing boards or state election officials abused their discretion in presiding over the counts? The latter standard establishes a very heavy burden on a plaintiff; the former wipes the slate clean of much of what happened during the protest period, even if the actions of election officials were perfectly correct.

As promised, Boies came to court Monday with a motion to begin counting the approximately 9,000 remaining Miami-Dade undervotes. Regarding their relevance, the Boies motion maintained that "if the remaining 9,000 uncounted undervote ballots result in the same proportional increase in net votes as the ballots that were counted by the Board before it stopped counting, these ballots would result in approximately 600 net additional votes for Gore/Lieberman." Enough, of course, to change the election outcome. Further, "Any effective legal relief will require the remaining undervote ballots themselves, which are the 'best evidence' of how the voters voted, to be counted."[4]

Moreover, according to Boies, time was of the essence:

> The work required to complete the vote count in Miami-Dade County must begin now to ensure that any judicial relief rendered in this proceeding will be timely. The counting of these ballots, already improperly delayed, cannot await the final resolution of the legal issues in this contest if the unique electoral college deadline imposed by Federal law is to be met. If a completed count of these ballots must await the prior resolution of these legal proceedings, there could very well be insufficient time to carry out this task and vindicate any relief ordered by this court.[5]

In light of subsequent events, one might be tempted to compliment Boies for his prescience. Beck and Terrell could not help but wonder why Boies seemed so insistent on planting this date, December 12, as the point of no return. However, they would do nothing to change that notion by arguing that the proceedings could well stretch to December 18—when the electoral college met—or even beyond with no reasonable prospect of calamity. Instead, Richard merely argued that to grant the Boies motion would be to provide Gore with the relief he sought without first establishing his legal right to that relief.

Judge Sauls denied the motion, whereupon Boies appealed that interim order directly to the Florida Supreme Court, which also denied relief. If Boies was going to get those ballots counted, he would have to do it after prevailing on the merits of his case.

"That's the way he played it and he had to live by the results," Terrell later recalled. But what would have happened if

Boies had simply asked for access to the undercount ballots for purposes of having his expert witness interpret them and then to introduce them into evidence? "Now that might have given us trouble," Terrell acknowledged.

Boies shunned this direct approach either because it was too simple to engage his brilliant, complex mind or because he had some reason for thinking he would not get the court to concur. Instead, he continued to press for a decision granting access regardless of what had gone before. "The fact that those votes exist is what is important, not whether or not they were certified, and not even whether or not they should have been certified," ran Boies's argument.[6]

Richard was at his best in reply to the Boies opening statement. What Boies demanded, Richard said, is "both unreasonable and contrary to Florida law. That this court should disregard all of the actions of the various canvassing boards that are under challenge here, and should begin anew an assessment and a count of all the votes that the plaintiffs challenge."[7]

"What then are the canvassing boards for?" Richard continued. If Boies is right, there was no need to count the votes election night. Gore and his team had to show that the boards abused their discretion, that they "acted in a fashion which no reasonable person could have done, given the facts known to them at the time."

If Boies was off to a shaky start in his argument, his case got worse as his witnesses took the stand. Kimball W. Brace, an election data consultant, tried to make the case that the Votomatic machines create problems through the buildup of chads over the voting holes as the voters fail to fully dislodge the paper. However, punching holes proved to be so easy that as Brace tried to demonstrate the making of dimples, his stylus punched right through.[8] As to the buildup of chads from voters incapable of punching holes, Beck asked sarcastically, "So as long as you got one big brute every 20 people or so that was actually able to vote, whatever chads are in there are going to get pushed off to the side, right?"

"Well there's a trough that they go into," replied Brace, his testimony wounded.[9]

Boies was trying to show that imperfections in the voting machine could explain how a voter intending to vote for Gore could leave a dimple instead of a hole, thus padding the case for interpreting dimples as reflecting intent. But the remedy—a manual recount—could create errors of its own. Beck, for example, confronted the witness with a National Bureau of Standards publication that warned that chads may be unintentionally "loosened in the handling" or through "lack of care in tearing off the stub of the chad."

Brace completed his testimony having done little or nothing for Gore. But compared to Gore's second and final witness, Yale Department of Statistics Professor Nicholas Hengartner, Brace had been a star.

Gore attorney Jeffrey Robinson took Hengartner on an excursion of recovery rates—the percentage of undervote ballots on which intent could be discerned under the particular standard being employed by the canvassing board. It was 26 percent in Broward County, and 22 percent in Miami-Dade, but only eight percent in Palm Beach. Beck saw the development of those numbers as more helpful to Bush than Gore. Rather than affirming the need for revised standards in Palm Beach, it helped confirm the critical point that the recount was a random, standardless operation, denying due process to the candidate at risk.

Hengartner's statistics were no more helpful to Gore than Brace's. Asked by Robinson how the new votes produced by recounts tended to break down, the witness replied that "the votes that were uncovered seemed to follow in the same proportions than [sic] the ones that the machines counted previously."[10] That played right into Beck's hands. Starting from scratch, Hengartner's crude projection could be of some use to Gore, because he had carried Miami-Dade County. But with the recount thus far limited to overwhelmingly Gore precincts, the balance of the undervotes would almost certainly favor Bush, thus undercutting the rationale for performing the exercise.

Hengartner's worst moment was still to come. In a sworn affidavit, part of the Gore team's proffer in support of their effort to get the counting started early, Hengartner had referred to the state elections of 1998, which involved contests for both the U.S. Senate and Governor. More Floridians had voted in the gubernatorial contest. The probable reason, according to Hengartner's sworn statement, was that the senatorial race appeared in column one of the ballot and the gubernatorial contest appeared in column two, and that the system apparently had not recorded all of the votes cast in column one. Although this would have reinforced Gore's claim that either a chad buildup or rubber erosion was responsible for some of the dimples, it was a high-risk, low-payoff line of attack because the Florida Supreme Court had already held that no machine or computer error was necessary to justify a manual recount. To the contrary, the court had specifically overruled Katherine Harris on this point, holding that even voter error could justify the search for voter intent.

What's more, Hengartner had gotten his facts wrong. Producing a sample 1998 ballot, which he highlighted on a screen for all to see, Beck picked up the cross-examination:

Q: Read, please, for the court, because this is out of focus, what is the race here up at the top of column one?

A: This is the congressional United States Senator.

Q: And then what's right underneath the United States Senator in column one?

A: State Governor and Lieutenant Governor.

Q: So what you said in your sworn affidavit was in column two was actually in column one, right?

A: It was the second race.

Q: Was it in column one on that ballot or not?

A: My understanding, it was the second race, and it should have been in column one, a mistake, it was the second race, and that's what I meant.

Q: Well, in your affidavit, you didn't say it was the fact that it was the second race is what's important. You said that the fact that the senate was column one, and the governor was in column two, why, that seemed to suggest that the voting machine wasn't recording all the votes cast in column one, because the guys in column two were getting more votes? Do you remember that?

A: I said that this was possible, yes.

Q: And you can see here that that sworn affidavit of yours, as well as the proffer that the lawyers submitted to this Court, and the Florida Supreme Court, that just wasn't true, was it?

A: It contained a mistake.

Q: And as you said it, notwithstanding what your affidavit said about a closer inspection of the ballot, you never even looked at the ballot, right?

A: I've looked at the order in which the races were ran [*sic*], sir.

Q: And when you signed that sworn statement, you were relying on the Gore legal team to give you the straight facts, weren't you?

A: Well, I relied on the facts that I received, yes.

As in their effort to convert the Pullen case in Illinois into precedent for counting dimpled chads, the Boies team had put false information before the court in an affidavit swearing that the information was true. It was, at best, extremely careless lawyering.

Boies then told the court he would put no more witnesses on the stand. This surprised both Beck and Terrell. Given the likelihood that Judge Sauls would make Gore meet the "reasonable probability" standard in order to get his manual recount, they had expected Gore to mount more of an evidentiary case. Gore had offered no evidence to suggest that the Miami-Dade decision to stop counting was wrong, or that inappropriate counting standards were used in Palm Beach County, or for that matter, that anything inappropriate was done in Nassau County, beyond merely asserting that it was.

Beck had also been surprised at what he would later describe as the "ridiculously dismal quality of the expert witnesses" Boies had placed on the stand. "This was professionally offensive to me in an important case," he recalled. "Their quality was similar to what you would get in a 'strike suit' product liability case where you put a lousy expert on the stand and then try to extract a settlement."

Beck and Terrell shared the view that Boies should have gone for the big hit by himself counting a sampling of undercount ballots and introducing the results as evidence interpreted by a qualified expert witness. By insisting that Sauls count them and appealing his refusal to the State Supreme Court, Boies had painted himself into a corner on the question of time while securing no relief.

As the Gore team concluded its case, Terrell glanced across the room at David Leahy, the Miami-Dade election commissioner whom he assumed would be a witness for Gore. True, he might have said some things about the suspension of the count that Gore might not have liked, but he might also have defended the way the ballots had been looked at in producing a 22 percent recovery rate. He might have explained how manual recounts could be conducted without degrading the ballots. He might have given a human face to the "count every vote" Gore slogan by showing how, with patience and diligence, it could actually produce a fair result. Why hadn't Boies called Leahy? Terrell thought the reason was uncertainty because he, Terrell, had initially placed Leahy on the Bush witness list, just in case he were needed to justify the November 22 decision to suspend the recount.

The Bush team was confident that Gore had failed to make a reasonable case for contesting the certification and they counted on their witnesses to put an exclamation point to the proceedings. As he had before Judge Labarga in Palm Beach County, Judge Charles Burton made a superb witness, brimming with common sense, an ethic of public responsibility, and by now, a practical familiarity with the vagaries of machine-made dimples and manual recounts. Why did he eventually opt for a conservative approach that disallowed most of the dimples? Simply because he experimented with the voting machines himself and found it hard to credit the notion of widespread inability to follow directions and punch holes. He recalled that prior to his testimony on November 22 before Judge Labarga, "I was asked to bring along a voting machine, and I tried it before, and it was very difficult to make an indentation like that, because it seemed it was quite easy for me to pop out the chad."[11]

One of the more revealing moments of the contest trial occurred when Burton was explaining his opposition to the standardless count that the board had undertaken in the sample precincts and his initially unsuccessful effort to impose more rigorous procedures. "Since that day I guess I've been the one accused of trying to block this recount, which is not the case," said Burton.

"Absolutely not," drawled Sauls from the bench. "I'll have to salute you as a great American."[12] There seemed little danger of the court disowning Burton's methodology, or his results.

Beck put his own expert witness, statistician Laurentius Marais, on the stand to clean up the statistical mess left by Boies and Hengartner. Recalling the Gore assertion that Miami-Dade could generate an additional 600 net Gore votes if the pattern established by the intial manual recount was continued by the remaining 9,000 undervote ballots, Beck questioned Marais.

Q: Now is that approach that is laid out in the Gore-Lieberman complaint a valid one from a statistical point of view?

A: It is not, and it makes for an unreliable and inaccurate projection, because it is based on a false premise.

Q: What is the false premise?

A: The false premise is stated in the portion of the text that you read. That is, if the proportion of net votes gained by the Gore side were the same in the remaining, approximately 9,000, then a certain result would follow.

But to interpret that and assess it, one needs to know that the portion of the precincts that were recounted by hand were heavily Democratic, in fact, those are precincts in which Gore won over Bush by a margin of greater than 75 percent to 25 percent.

That is very different from the remaining precincts where, in fact, in the underlying machine recount totals, Bush beats Gore by a margin of about 52 to 48 percent.[13]

Beck had faced one interesting dilemma in attempting to rebut Hengartner's testimony to the effect that the high percentage of undervotes in Palm Beach County—2.2 percent—suggested problems with the Votomatic machines there. Beck knew an alternative explanation: voters were confused by the butterfly ballots in that county and had made all sorts of random marks while deciding how to vote for the presidential candidate of their choice. Convincing? Perhaps, but it would certainly reinforce the complaint of Gore supporters that the butterfly ballot had been responsible for their man losing Florida.

Beck raised the matter with Ben Ginsberg, who told him to use the confusion explanation if it would help his contest case. After all, the butterfly lawsuits were failing on every front. The presidency would likely be decided in the contest trial. Now was not the time to be erecting monuments to consistency, or the next monument erected could be a memorial to the Bush candidacy.

Armed with Ginsberg's approval, Beck asked the witness whether the confusing ballot, rather than rubber or other machine problems, could be the reason why people either didn't vote at all or "claim they were so confused by the ballot that they ended up voting for two people?"

"It's one of the things one would want to consider," Marais replied.

Q: And would you also want to consider, if you were going to do thorough investigation, that there were other people who claim that they were confused by the ballot and they ended up voting for the wrong guy?

A: That would suggest another explanation to be investigated, yes sir.

Q: So would you want to investigate whether there was a possibility that with that same butterfly ballot that people complained about, some people might have just thrown their hands up in the air and said, "I can't figure this out, I'm not going to vote for any of these guys"?

A: It would be a factor to consider.[14]

Not all of the Bush team moves were as inspired. John Ahmann, a former IBM engineer who had updated that company's Votomatic machine and who held patents on later machines, was called to rebut the notion that machine failure had been responsible for many of the undervotes even though this was a matter of complete irrelevancy under the first of the Florida Supreme Court decisions. "I seriously doubt that the voter would be unable to push the chad through on a normal voting device," he testified.[15] Later he rejected the claim that most dimples represent attempts to vote for the candidate near whose name it appears. Instead, "An indentation may result from a voter placing the stylus in the position, but not punching through."[16]

Ahmann also found unimpressive the Gore claim that chad buildup could somehow prevent the stylus from punching through. "I know of no way it could happen," he said.[17]

So far, so good. But Steven Zack, one of the Gore lawyers, immediately began to cross-examine Ahmann on a patent application he had filed in 1982 for an automatic voting machine designed to eliminate some of the problems with its predecessors, models that happened to have been used in those Florida counties that still relied on the punch-card method. The Bush lawyers exchanged nervous glances. None had known about the patent application Zack was talking about.

They would soon learn about it. In describing the old machines, the application stated: "Therefore, the material typically used for punch board and punch card voting can and does contribute to potentially unreadable votes because of hanging chad or mispunched cards."[18]

Another problem identified on the application: "If chips are permitted to accumulate between the resilient strips, this can interfere with the punching operations. . . . Incompletely punched cards can cause serious errors to occur."

Moreover, both in deposition and on the witness stand, Ahmann agreed with one of the central Gore contentions: Zack asked, "In close elections a hand recount is advisable, correct?" Ahmann replied, "In very close elections, yes."[19]

Beck was embarrassed but not particularly troubled by the Ahmann admissions. Clearly, it had changed the ambiance in the courtroom from one of an untrammeled Bush march to victory to something rather less. Legally speaking, however, Beck would later call it a "nonevent." Recounts, after all, were not the central issue. Gore had requested and received recounts in only four counties. The issue was the disposition of those recounts by the canvassing boards whose actions were now in dispute. If the court adopted Boies's reasoning that their actions were irrelevant and the closeness of the election per se entitled Gore to the recounts of his choice, then very little that had gone on in the court would matter. If, on the other hand, Gore had to prove by a reasonable preponderance of the evidence that the boards had abused their discretion and that more counting was likely to change the results, he had failed miserably. His statistics were flawed and his evidence nonexistent. Despite all the talk about uneven rubber wear and chad buildup, Boies hadn't offered a shred of evidence of a single machine malfunction.

The remaining witnesses covered other bases of the Bush position: The counting techniques varied from county to county, and in the case of Miami-Dade, from one canvassing board member to another. The Miami-Dade sampling was egregiously weighted in favor of heavily Democratic precincts. Voters in non-recount counties had their votes diluted by the manual recounts. A voter who had started to vote for Gore and changed his mind, intending in the end to cast no vote for president, testified he was certain he had left a dimpled chad next to Gore's name. Shirley King, the supervisor of elections for Nassau County, gave a matter-of-fact recitation of the "lost" 218 presidential votes, which she had corrected via procedures so open and aboveboard that one could feel the sting going out of the Gore complaint. The Bush team offered no evidence to challenge the counting techniques employed in Broward County, in part because their collective judgment was that Gore had presented too weak a case to require it and in part because they felt there might still be time to offer "remedial" evidence if Gore did prevail.

Like Beck, Terrell suffered a moment of embarrassment. Paul Spargo, a Republican election lawyer from Albany, New York, came to Miami on November 18 to assist in monitoring the actions of the board. He testified about the process of "chad mutilation" attendant to the counting and at one point claimed to have seen at least a thousand loose chad pieces on the floor, all the product of a single day's counting. Regarding the condition of the ballots, Spargo said, "Well, the handling of them, at least the ones that have been counted, are—have been subjected to a lot of mishandling, if you will, to the extent they've been impounded, they've been twisted, they've been moved around, rubbed up against each other, and I think, to many degrees, to the extent that new chad has accumulated, those ballots have been substantially changed."[20]

Not the testimony on which the election would likely hinge, thought Terrell, but a useful fleshing out of the Bush position that new manual recounts would as likely be a source of mischief as enlightenment.

But the second question from Gore lawyer Kendall Coffey almost knocked Terrell off his chair. "Isn't it true," Coffey began, "that the last time you were on the witness stand on matters of reliability and integrity in an election scenario, you took the Fifth Amendment nineteen times?"[21]

Terrell leapt to his feet. "This is what you call your basic bushwhack," he complained. "He knows it's not proper. He's coming in to embarrass him [Spargo] and I suggest he tender whatever evidence he's got. I think it's irrelevant."

Technically Terrell knew he was right. Spargo had never been convicted of anything and had faced no disciplinary proceeding with the New York State Bar Association or the courts over the incident, which had occurred more than a decade ago. The question was out of order and, after a short conference in chambers, Judge Sauls ruled the issue closed. Still, Terrell hadn't known a thing about it, and that bothered him. Plus the bolt from the blue had again unsettled what had been a long and smooth Bush run.

For reasons that were not evident at the time and are no more apparent today, Beck decided against introducing evidence to challenge the liberal counting rules of Broward County which had netted Gore 567 votes. Beck would later maintain that he knew Gore's case had failed and decided to let well enough alone. But the decision seems one of those mistakes from which lucky lawyers escape unharmed and unlucky ones—or at least their clients—suffer. With nothing on the record to support the claim of poor methodology, the state supreme court was quite correct when, days later, it considered the recount results final and exempted Broward County from the statewide recount it ordered. Had the U.S. Supreme Court then remanded the Florida ruling with instructions to resume the recount under a single counting standard, it too could have exempted Broward County as settled. As gifted as was his destruction of the Gore expert witnesses, Beck left slightly ajar a door to disaster that readily could have been closed.

Little in the closing argument of either side could be characterized as particularly noteworthy. The lawyers had made the central points in briefs and opening statements and there was now little left to say. Richard, in his closing argument for Bush, did try to distinguish the protest and contest periods on the issue of voter error and intent. Whatever rule the state supreme court had applied to the protest period, he argued, voter error could not possibly be a basis for overturning a certified election. That would be like a voter saying that because he forgot to vote on election day, he was entitled to have the polls opened for his benefit sometime later.

A lawyer named William Jenkins, who had represented five individual Bush supporters, did offer in his closing argument perhaps the most candid statement of Bush's opposition to manual recounts from Day One of the battle: "Governor Bush got his undergraduate degree from Yale University, Your Honor, he got an MBA from Harvard, he's been successful in many businesses. I suggest to the Court that there is absolutely no way that he is going to ask for any recount in the statewide election that he already won."[22]

By the time the last lawyer had finished the last argument before Judge Sauls, it was 11 P.M. on Sunday, December 3, and the parties had spent 14 hours of their day in court. Despite the mental and physical fatigue, the Bush camp was optimistic. They had been bitter when Gore had announced his intention to contest the certification. Even Bush, in a private conversation with Baker had expressed "shock" that Gore "will not stop at anything." To Bush, who rarely personalizes his political battles, Gore had shown he had "no sense of decency." Now, the men and women who had worked to defeat Gore in the postelection battle felt he was about to get his comeuppance. "We were a little nervous, but we thought we had won," recalled Kenneth Juster. Phil Beck thought that "Gore had essentially presented no evidence to support his claims."

True enough, but as the hour for the Sauls decision drew near, MSNBC reported that twenty-five counting teams had been assembled at the circuit court. That could mean a decision for Gore, with the counting to begin immediately after its announcement. Bush lawyers shuddered at the thought and then rejected it as the body rejects a foreign organ: No, the case had gone too well. No trial court could hold against us on this record. Victory is at hand.

The taste of impending victory became stronger when the U.S. Supreme Court handed down its decision vacating the first Florida Supreme Court case. Then word came that Judge Sauls would announce his decision at 4 P.M. Walking to the courthouse, Fred Bartlit warned his colleagues to keep a poker face no matter what happened. As an old trial lawyer, he may have been a bit superstitious. Or he may have been thinking that there would still be legal battles ahead and he wanted no one to take offense at an arrogant Bush team celebration.

Sauls began reading his opinion. His recitation of the issues seemed to drag on forever, but after reviewing the Gore charges of mistakes and irregularities, he set the bar high: "It is not enough to show a reasonable possibility that election

results could have been altered by such irregularities or in-
accuracies. Rather, a reasonable probability that the results
of the election would have been changed must be shown."
Then came the clincher: "In this case, there is no credible statistical evidence and no other competent substantial evidence
to establish by a preponderance a reasonable probability
that the results of the statewide election in the state of
Florida would be different from the result which has been
certified by the State Elections Canvassing Commission."[23]

Sauls proceeded to find for Bush on every material issue:

• There is "no authority under Florida law for certification of an incomplete, manual recount of a portion of or less
than all ballots from any county."

• There is no authority to "include any returns submitted
past the deadline established by the Florida Supreme Court."

• Regardless of voter error or equipment problems, Gore
failed to show that a full recount in Miami-Dade County
would be likely to reverse the statewide outcome.

• There was no abuse of discretion—a necessary element
for Gore to succeed—by the canvassing boards.

• The Palm Beach County Canvassing Board had acted
within its discretion in establishing counting standards.

• A two-tier system giving voters in recount counties a
greater chance of having their ballots counted may well violate the equal protection clause.

• The Nassau County Canvassing Board acted properly in
substituting its election night ballot count for the inaccurate
mandatory machine recount figure. Moreover, had Gore sought
to challenge the result, he should have sought a recount.[24]

There were screams and cheers and high-fives all over the
GOP headquarters. Back at the court, one Bush lawyer scrib-
bled "Home Run" on his legal pad and handed it to a colleague. The colleague added his own postscript: "Total

Fucking Victory!" A more sober Phil Beck said, "This was as complete a victory as I've ever gotten at a trial."[25]

"They won. We lost. This is going to be resolved by the Florida Supreme Court," snapped Boies with unusual brevity. "I think whoever wins at the Florida Supreme Court, we'll accept that."[26]

Yes, the case would go to the Florida Supreme Court. The Bush lawyers knew that as well as anyone. Yet there was no discounting the importance of the Sauls decision. First and foremost, there had not been a single vote counted in Florida since November 26—eight days before—and none would be counted at least until after the Florida Supreme Court ordered recounts to resume. Gore was being backed up against a deadline. It may already be too late for him to prevail. And his ability to forge ahead in the recount, thereby preempting the Florida legislature, was destroyed.

Second, Sauls had found for Bush both on the law and on the facts. The Florida Supreme Court might have its own idea of the law, but they would owe considerable deference to the trial judge's finding of facts. And in any event, those facts, particularly regarding the weird and standardless counting procedures, would still be on the record, ready to influence the U.S. Supreme Court should it decide to hear arguments of equal protection and due process.

Third, as feisty as that supreme state tribunal had been in the past, it was now surrounded on three sides. The Sauls opinion had been based on an underlying factual record that would be hard to ignore. True, the judge's opinion amounted to little more than a series of sweeping statements and evidentiary findings without specific citation to the testimony on which it was based, but that record was there for a reviewing court to examine. And if that court chose to go off on another frolic of its own, the U.S. Supreme Court had just shown it was not reticent about vacating state Supreme Court decisions grounded in hyperactivism. Further, the Florida State Legislature was contemplating a special session to appoint a slate of Bush electors. With time desperately short, the state court still had one more move to make. Could it impose its naked will on the process? Probably not.

As he left the courthouse, Irv Terrell played the kind of mental game trial lawyers often play, putting themselves in the adversary's situation and thinking how they might have handled things had the roles been reversed. "I think David was so confident he'd get the results he wanted in the Florida Supreme Court that he never paid as much attention as he might have to building a good record," Terrell later recalled. "His approach was to throw spaghetti on the wall and see if it sticks. David thought he could win with a lot of confusion, a lot of chaos, and that with standardless counting he'd be okay." Boies, he felt, never built a good statistical case. And he was stretched very thin. The Bush team was organized into a group of strategic thinkers at the top, supported by trial lawyers and brief writers, plus the people who ran the ground war in the recount jurisdictions. Together they had beaten a team led by a talented superstar but with a supporting cast boasting few candidates for the litigation hall of fame. The Bush team was in good shape now. All they needed was one more win, and it could come from almost anywhere.

In fact, the odds looked so good that there was hopeful speculation that Gore might choose this moment to give up his battle. Baker remembered that Tom Feeney had by coincidence scheduled a press conference to discuss legislative plans to name a list of Bush electors. This was a poor moment for that. Baker liked and respected Feeney, but also saw him as a tough little burr who could easily get under the blanket of the Democratic donkey and turn its backside raw. This was one of the only times during the postelection battle for Florida that Baker called Feeney directly, asking him to hold off while everyone watched Washington for Gore's next move. Feeney agreed and postponed his conference.

Gore stayed in the fight.

CHAPTER 8

Losing in the State Court

Thursday, December 7. "Hear ye, hear ye, hear ye. The Supreme Court of the great state of Florida is now in session," cried the bailiff. He might have added, "And the presidency of the United States hangs in the balance." That unspoken thought seemed to humble Chief Justice Charles Wells as he began questioning David Boies at a session that would mark the beginning of five days of constitutional turmoil.

Should the Florida Supreme Court even be involved? Wells wondered. Didn't the U.S. Supreme Court rule just days ago that under a century-old precedent the state legislature has plenary power to provide for the selection of presidential electors? And hadn't the Florida legislature given the circuit court the power to resolve contest disputes with no reference at all to the supreme court's power of appellate review?

Both Boies and later Richard, representing Bush, seemed a bit nonplussed by the question. Neither had questioned the supreme court's power of appellate review as implicit in the process of judicial responsibility. In fact, with a touchy challenge to the absentee ballots of Seminole and Martin counties moving toward resolution in a circuit courtroom presided over by two unpredictable Democratic judges, the moment did not seem a propitious one in which to attack the

concept of appellate review. Still, the very question pro-
pounded by the chief justice suggested a far different atmos-
phere among the supreme court justices than the first time
around.

Justice Peggy Quince wondered why during the contest period Gore should be able to potentially overturn a statewide
election with selective county recounts. "And why wouldn't
it be proper for any court, if they're going to order any relief, to count the undervotes in all of the counties where, at
the very least, punch card systems were operating?"[1]

Boies had been facing variations on the same question
from the media and the courts since the outset of the protest
and his response was always a variation of his reply here: "I
think the first difference is that that's where the ballots were
contested."[2]

Boies further urged that Judge Sauls's decision had been
based on three errors of law. First, that there was a need for
a statewide recount; second, that the standard for judicial review was abuse of discretion by the canvassing boards; and
third, that in order for the court to inspect ballots, Gore had
first to show a reasonable probability that the result of a ballot recount would change the outcome of the election.

Justice Major B. Harding then hit Boies with the same
question Terrell had reflected about during the trial below.
"Did anyone ever pick up one of the ballots and hold it up
and show it to the judge and say, 'This is an example of a
ballot which was rejected but which a vote is reflected?'"[3]

Boies had no answer of consequence. At trial, he had simply put the ballots into evidence and urged the court to count
them.

Richard was also asked to address the question of whether
the court had jurisdiction to review the Sauls decision. "Indeed you do," he replied. "In fact this is nothing more than
a garden-variety appeal from a final judgment by a lower
court reviewed after a full evidentiary hearing."[4]

Among the Bush lawyers watching the argument in person
or on television back at GOP headquarters, that response,

more than any other single event, produced instant heart-burn and confirmed the suspicion of several that Richard was a glib but overrated ally. "Garden variety appeal," indeed! With the presidency of the United States up for grabs, the Gore team urging that what was involved was simply a state court interpreting state law, and constitutional scholars around the country debating whether there was a federal hook for U.S. Supreme Court intervention, the last thing in the world the Bush team wanted to be doing was trivializing the legal issues at stake. Rather than calling it "garden variety," it was in the interest of Governor George W. Bush to underline the fact that this was a unique and monumentally important case. At issue here was no county sheriff race, but one governed by a comprehensive federal scheme and strict rules passed by the state legislature, both of which severely proscribed the options of the state supreme court. No broad equitable powers could be invoked here, no muscling aside of legislative prerogatives. Change the law and your "safe harbor" is gone. Encroach on legislative mandates and you have trampled Article 2.

Justices Harry Lee Anstead and Barbara J. Pariente pushed Richard on the question of whether the trial judge had erred in refusing to review the ballots admitted into evidence. How, Justice Pariente asked, could Judge Sauls be said to have met the statutory mandate to "do whatever is necessary" to ensure that each allegation in the complaint is investigated without counting the ballots?

Here Richard's response was in the right direction: "We had an absolute failure on the part of plaintiffs here. This court gave the plaintiffs the opportunity to have a trial to prove their case, and it was an absolute failure in the record of this case to establish an abuse of discretion by any of the canvassing boards."[5]

Then, in a sustained question and riposte exchange with Justice Pariente regarding the undervotes in Miami-Dade County, Richard failed to emphasize the statistical problem with the Gore case. If the mere number of undervotes equal to or greater than the number of votes separating the candidates justifies a recount, then why did Gore's lawyers choose as one of their two witnesses a Yale statistician who sought to project a favorable recount outcome from what had been counted thus far? The reason was simply that he was trying to establish a case for the importance of a further recount. Due to Beck's withering cross-examination and effective testimony from a Bush rebuttal witness, the Gore team had failed miserably to do so. Not only was Judge Sauls on solid ground reaching that conclusion, but the evidence in the record against Gore's claim was so overwhelming, it might have constituted reversible error for Sauls to have gone the other way. Richard's failure to close that latch would let the Florida Supreme Court open the door to further mischief.

Richard also wandered back into the briar patch of voter error versus voter intent, claiming that for Gore to prevail, he had "to show that there was any reason to believe that any voter was denied the right to vote because of something other than the voter's own fault."[6] While the Florida Supreme Court in the first election case had specifically rebuked this standard, the issue had received continuing attention from the Bush lawyers. What standard should the courts or counters apply in determining whether a voter's less-than-perfect expression of his will should count? Terwilliger wanted no standard associated with the Bush forces; let the courts create their own problems. Beck urged backing for the Burton/Palm Beach County standard that dimpled chads don't count unless their pattern suggests voter intent. Terrell himself urged what he called the "statutory compliance" standard, that without proof that the voter sought to comply with directions to punch the hole with his stylus, his vote should be discarded.

At some point the issues merged. The more tolerant the standard for counting, the more undervotes would become votes for one candidate or the other. The more votes for one candidate or the other, the greater the likelihood a manual recount would alter the outcome of the battle. Ironically, what the Bush lawyers never appreciated was that once Gore had skimmed the cream off his four selected counties, Bush had more to gain than lose by tolerant counting rules everywhere else. Contrary to the belief of the state GOP, subsequent recounts would show that Republicans were scarcely more immune than Democrats to voter error. The stylus proved a nonpartisan instrument of iniquity. In counties where there were more Republicans, there were more recoverable Republican votes.

Not until the closing moments of his argument did Richard return to the salient point of Gore's failure to sustain any burden of proof at trial. To order a new recount, he said, the court must conclude that such a recount would change the result of the election. "If you look at the evidence here and you look at the lower court judge's determination, no matter which standard you use, there was insufficient evidence to indicate that," said Richard.[7]

From his place at the counsel table where he was once again representing Katherine Harris, Joe Klock found the proceedings faintly ironic. Here was a court dealing with at least three different counting standards, none of which had been in place prior to November 7, each of which therefore violated the "safe harbor" federal law provision that the U.S. Supreme Court only days ago had urged the state court to respect. The same was true with the selective county recount. Even this court now seemed to recognize it as constitutionally offensive. Yet how could they change? "The Florida Supreme Court was caught between Sylla and Charybdis," Klock would later say. "If they don't articulate new standards both as regards ballot counting and having the recount go statewide, they run afoul of equal protection. If they do make the standards conform to equal protection, they have changed the law in violation of 3 U.S.C. § 5 and probably Article 2 as well. Particularly after the U.S. Supreme Court had warned the Florida court not to tamper with the safe harbor, they had nowhere to go." In his brief argument, Klock simply warned the court that should it decide to reverse Judge

Sauls and conduct new recounts, it would likely run afoul of the "safe harbor" warning "because the problem is that you have to create a pile of law to do it."[8]

In his final argument Boies showed himself at his most dexterous and arrogant. The dexterity involved the Miami-Dade recount. Under a statute that plainly on its face requires a recount of "all the ballots," Chief Justice Wells asked how the court, without legislating from the bench, could order only the 9,000 undervotes counted.

Boies's reply: "But I think that's right, Your Honor. I think that you could interpret the law that way. I think you could also interpret the law in the sense of saying all the ballots that were requested to be manually recounted. If neither party requested the others to be manually recounted, and if the machine was recording votes, I don't think you would necessarily, under that statute, have to interpret it that you would have to do that."[9]

Of course, Boies had reason to feel confident that a majority of Florida justices would interpret clear statutory provisions as meaning the opposite of their plain definitions. Just two weeks earlier the same court had done so in writing new deadlines for completing manual recounts.

Finally, Boies once again was asked to defend recounting the ballots in four Democratic counties but ignoring those counties that voted heavily for Bush. Boies replied that "every party has a right to contest, but no party is required to contest. What the sense seems to be is that somehow Governor Bush's campaign should be protected from Governor Bush's lawyers. If they didn't ask for a recount, and therefore, there should be a recount anyway, even if they didn't ask for it."[10]

Boies's smug put-down of the Bush lawyers was as legally flawed as it was inappropriate. Although any party can request a recount in the early protest period, only the losing candidate can contest a recount following certification. Thus even if Bush had sought to reverse an election he had won, Florida state law would have prevented him from doing so.

Why the certified victor would undertake such an effort is a question that would tax even the subtle and complex intellect of David Boies.

The Bush team had mixed feelings about the Florida Supreme Court argument. One certainly sensed a thirst for closure, a disinclination to disturb the judgment of the lower court among a few of the justices. Even the more activist justices could provide no real answer to the question of how any new recount could be accomplished by the December 12 deadline, now less than five days away. Finally, there was a sense that Richard had not enjoyed his best day. He had mentioned the court's limited jurisdiction, but not really driven the point home. He had not been particularly effective in responding to Boies's erroneous claim that the completed recount in Palm Beach County produced a net gain of 215 votes for Gore rather than the correct figure, 174. He had not been powerful enough in emphasizing that permitting the figures from Miami-Dade's partial recount to stand would violate the equal protection clause if not the Voting Rights Act of 1965.

How much of this concern was rational and how much was the product of fatigue, tension, frustration, jealousy, and political bias is tough to judge. Clearly, December 7 had not been Richard's finest day as an attorney, any more than November 20 had been Michael Carvin's. But this was a court that followed its own zealous instincts, controlling through questions from the bench the issues counsel could fruitfully address.

Still the conversation at GOP headquarters continued. From the course of the argument there was agreement that at least three justices—Wells, Harding and Shaw—seemed likely to vote to affirm the decision of the lower court. Pariente and Anstead were hopeless. Quince had some problems with equal protection and Lewis was a mystery. Maybe there was some way to get one last thought before the court that might sway a wavering justice for the vote needed to put George W. Bush in the White House.

The discussion turned to Wells's opening questions on jurisdiction. Clearly some reminder of the limited nature of the court's function was called for. But what about the contest statute itself? Did it really apply to presidential contests? In earlier proceedings the Bush team had conceded that it did, as ill-suited as it was for any statewide race. Some on the Bush team had continued to question its applicability and it had only been at the eleventh hour that they had decided not to argue against contests in their motion to dismiss the Gore complaint before Judge Sauls.

Now Bolton, Juster, and others suggested that the group begin to write something that might be filed as a supplementary brief to the state supreme court case just argued. In its final form the short supplemental brief would include sections on the court's jurisdiction, the Palm Beach count, Miami-Dade, and the supposed nonapplicability of the contest option to a presidential election. In a sharp footnote to its December 8 decision, the court called attention to the "substantial and dramatic change of position after oral argument in this case," and the fact that the new Bush position had been expressly disowned by both Carvin and Richard in their respective arguments before the court.[11] Indeed, Carvin in open court had argued that a principal reason not to extend the initial certification deadline would be to avoid stepping on the contest period where Gore could make his case to the courts. Not only did the switch fail to attract an additional vote on the court, but also it provided a foul whiff of legal opportunism to what otherwise had been a compelling case. "It was something we did in haste and under incredible time constraints," one Bush lawyer later explained. "And while I think there is merit to the contention that Florida's contest provisions are unworkable in the presidential context, in light of our previous positions, it would have been better not to have introduced the argument at the time and in the way we did."

Still some of the Bush lawyers remained confident. The combination of the Sauls decision and the first ruling by the

U.S. Supreme Court, together with a sense in the media that the Gore effort was entering its final days, had produced a feeling of mild euphoria among many. About the only blip on the screen had been that on December 6, the 11th Circuit Court of Appeals had voted 8–4 to again deny Bush's motion to stop the recount on the grounds that it had not caused him "irrevocable harm," because he had been certified the winner despite the recount. That decision had been widely expected and, again, had not affected the merits of the challenge to the Florida recount. Now that the ground wars had been fought, briefs written, and the cases argued, the end of the fight seemed at hand. Lawyers and laymen to whom 18-hour days had become a way of life now reestablished contacts with families and loved ones. Serious packing got underway. Departures began and soon evolved into a rather substantial exodus. Even an adverse Florida Supreme Court decision would likely affect only three or four counties. The core of the task force remained in place, but most others could head for home.

Early in the afternoon of December 8, Judges Nikki Ann Clark and Terry P. Lewis rejected Democratic claims in Seminole and Martin counties respectively, allowing the absentee ballots to stand and ending a lethal if long-shot threat to the Bush certification. The Gore campaign was now down to its last hope. In Washington, Gore, who had insisted publicly that his chances of winning were "50–50," and Lieberman later disclosed that they had gone to work on concession statements. Instead of delivering them, however, the two Democrats received an eleventh-hour reprieve from the Florida Supreme Court. As a joyful David Boies told his client and the television cameras, "Four to three is better than 50–50."[12]

The unsigned opinion held that Judge Sauls had erred in refusing to count the 9,000 undervotes in Miami-Dade County, in failing to add to Gore's total the 168 votes picked up during the suspended Miami-Dade recount, and in supporting the secretary of state's refusal to accept the late-filed recounted ballots from Palm Beach County. It ordered the counting of the Miami-Dade undervotes to begin immediately and, to skirt equal protection problems, a manual statewide recount of all undervotes to begin on Saturday, the following morning.

The court affirmed Judge Sauls's refusal to question the counting techniques of Judge Burton and his Palm Beach colleagues, and his rejection of Gore's challenge to the Nassau County certification of its election night count rather than the erroneous mandatory machine recount.

The court made a perfunctory effort to address concerns raised by the U.S. Supreme Court decision it had yet to respond to, quoting the 3 U.S.C. § 5 requirement that the election be determined by procedures in place before the vote, and claiming its decision was based solely on statutes on the books before November 7.

Gore's challenge rested on the "rejection of a number of legal votes sufficient to change or place in doubt the result of the election." On the basis of no case law whatsoever, the court overturned Sauls's ruling that, to prevail, the plaintiffs must prove that the canvassing boards abused their discretion regarding which votes to count. Instead, it held that "the board's actions concerning the elections process may constitute evidence in a contest proceeding," a far easier barrier for Gore to overcome.[13]

The court also found that a plain reading of the statute refuted Sauls's conclusion that all votes must be counted in a contest proceeding. Instead, only the ballots challenged for having been illegal but counted or legal but not counted need be assessed. However, the court stated that Gore's selective recount strategy could not limit the remedy:

> We do agree, however, that it is absolutely essential in this proceeding and to any final decision that a manual recount be conducted for all legal votes in this State, not only in Miami-Dade County, but in all Florida counties where there was an undervote, and hence a concern that not every citizen's vote was counted. This election should be determined by a careful examination of the votes of Florida's citizens and not by strategies extraneous to the voting process.[14]

Regarding the burden of proof, the court, employing what can most charitably be described as an awesome contempt for judicial precedent, held that Sauls had erroneously required Gore to show "a reasonable probability" that the undercount ballots would have changed the result. Instead, it held that the 1999 contest law required only a number of undervotes "sufficient to change or place in doubt" the results, despite the fact that the legislative history made it plain that the legislature had intended only to codify existing law.

Then what must a challenger show? According to the Florida court, only that a sufficient number of undervotes exist "which, if cast for the unsuccessful candidate, would change or place in doubt the result of the election."[15] To fully appreciate the weirdness of this new judicial formulation, take the case where Gore was trailing by 570 votes with 10,750 undervotes still at issue in Miami-Dade County. Assuming a "recovery rate" of 22 percent legal votes—the actual Miami-Dade experience—an additional 1,265 legal votes would be recovered, or more than twice the number needed to satisfy the new Florida Supreme Court standard. Assume further that the newly discovered votes break down similar to the vote recorded November 7 in the county, 52 percent for Gore and 47 percent for Bush. Then, on the basis of reasonable statistical projection, Gore could expect to receive about 658 additional votes from the county, and Bush an additional 595. The net Gore pick-up of 63 votes was almost precisely what independent counters found months later using the most liberal counting techniques. Had the Florida Supreme Court employed even the most basic concepts of statistical analysis, it would have concluded that Gore not only failed to meet the "reasonable probability" standard articulated by Judge Sauls, but that the likelihood of his overtaking the Bush statewide lead with a big showing in Miami-Dade resided somewhere in the most remote regions of the bell-shaped curve. Yet this was the standard the court declared had been embraced by a 1999 law the legislature believed simply codified existing standards.

Of all the elements of the state supreme court decision, Phil Beck found this to be the dead giveaway of the court's lack of balance. "If the Florida Supreme Court had its way, a disappointed candidate could always get a recount if the number of undercounted votes was greater than the difference between him and the winner," he later noted. "And that's absurd."

After next proclaiming, as it implicitly had in its earlier *Gore v. Harris* decision, that "a legal vote is one in which there is a 'clear indication of the intent of the voter,'"[16] the court said Judge Sauls had committed reversible error "by failing to examine the specifically identified group of uncounted ballots that is claimed to contain the rejected legal votes." In the view of the court, "The trial court has presented the plaintiffs with the ultimate catch-22, acceptance of the only evidence that will resolve the issue but a refusal to examine such evidence."[17]

This was a crudely worded if not thoroughly intemperate misstatement of what Sauls had done. Sauls did not randomly refuse to examine the ballots. Rather, as is routinely done at trials, he demanded that Gore establish a predicate for its introduction with credible statistical projections that the undervotes would be meaningful. Boies understood the rules. Why else would he have brought a statistician to make those projections under oath? But Beck's cross-examination and the testimony of a rebuttal expert witness destroyed the testimony of Boies's statistician. Even then, had Boies been on top of his game, he would have sought to restore the importance of the ballots by allowing an expert witness to inspect some of them and testify regarding their ability to reverse the certified election result. For reasons best known to himself, Boies never sought to go that route. Rather than "the ultimate catch-22," Boies had received his day in court and had suffered a simple failure of evidence.

The court next found error in Sauls's failure to count 215 votes from Palm Beach County allegedly certified by county officials after the 5 P.M. November 26 deadline—a deadline established by the state supreme court itself in the first *Gore v. Harris* case. The 215 figure was erroneous, the apparent product of Judge Burton's faulty recollection at the contest trial and repeated by Boies with glee long after the error had been called to his attention.[18] The more interesting question, however, is not the staying power of this faulty figure, but how the court found its way around its own clear deadline. Said the majority: "The deadline was never intended to prohibit legal votes identified after that date through ongoing manual recounts to be excluded from the statewide official results in the election canvassing commission's certification of the results of a recount of less than all of a county's ballots."[19] If the words seem indecipherable, the logic is no more clear.

Because Gore had introduced no evidence to dispute the counting techniques employed by Palm Beach County, and had demanded no recount in Nassau County, the court found for Bush on these two issues.

That left the matter of the 168 net votes Gore had picked up in the heavily Democratic precincts of Miami-Dade County prior to the canvassing board's decision to stop counting. Astonishingly, the state supreme court held that Gore was entitled to these votes, which by any sane analysis tended more to distort than reflect the Miami-Dade vote. The stated rationale was that these were "legal votes and these votes could change the outcome of the election."[20] But counting them presented a grossly distorted picture of the Miami-Dade vote.

"The Florida Supreme Court showed its bias by ordering a complete recount except where Gore had already won," Beck later observed. "It was ludicrous."

The court ordered the Miami-Dade recount of remaining undervotes to begin at once with the statewide undervote recount to begin at 8 A.M. the following morning. The canvassing boards could retain extra help, if necessary, in the counting. The court majority hoped to see all ballots counted, all ballot disputes resolved, and all judicial appeals exhausted in four days. In a footnote, the majority conceded the near impossibility of the ordered undertaking. "While we agree that practical difficulties may well end up controlling the outcome of the election we vigorously disagree that we should therefore abandon our responsibility to resolve this election dispute under the rule of law."[21]

The opinion of the court majority contained not a single reference to the U.S. Supreme Court decision of just four days earlier. Neither had the court revised its earlier opinion in light of the expressed U.S. Supreme Court concerns. Both in manner and in substance, the majority justices of Florida seemed intent on playing an "in-your-face" brand of jurisprudence that invited critical review by the nation's highest tribunal.

Chief Justice Wells and Justices Harding and Shaw dissented. Writing for himself alone, the Chief Justice warned, "the majority's decision cannot withstand the scrutiny which will certainly immediately follow under the United States Constitution." Justice Wells wrote

> The majority returns the case to the circuit court for this partial recount of undervotes on the basis of unknown or, at best, ambiguous standards with authority to obtain help from others, the credentials, qualifications, and objectivity of whom is totally unknown. That is but a first glance at the imponderable problems the majority creates.
>
> Importantly to me, I have a deep and abiding concern that the prolonging of judicial process in this counting contest propels this country and this state into an unprecedented and unnecessary constitutional crisis.[22]

In the absence of "dishonesty, gross negligence, improper influence, coercion, or fraud in the balloting and counting processes," the test must be abuse of discretion on the part of the canvassing boards. Here, wrote Wells, the majority has ordered a manual recount simply because Gore has charged that "enough legal votes were rejected to place in doubt the results of the election. Following this logic to its conclusion would require a circuit court to order partial manual recounts upon the mere filing of a contest. This proposition plainly has no basis in the law."[23]

Chief Justice Wells articulated three additional problems with the majority opinion that would prove prescient. First, in a footnote he wondered why only undervotes—ballots on which no vote for the presidency were recorded—would be recounted while overvotes—ballots disqualified because two or more presidential votes were observed—were left to stand. In Palm Beach County a name with a punch hole through it trumped one with a mere dimple. In counties where there had been no manual recount, those same ballots would have been excluded.

Second, Wells wrote, "I conclude it is plain error for the majority to hold that the Commission abused its discretion in enforcing a deadline set by the Court that recounts be completed and certified by November 26, 2000. I conclude that this not only changes a rule after November 7, 2000, but it also changes a rule this Court made on November 26, 2000."[24]

Finally, the court had let stand vastly different counting rules in different counties:

> Should a county canvassing board count or not count a "dimpled chad" where the voter is able to successfully dislodge the chad in every other contest on that ballot? Here, the county canvassing boards disagree. Apparently, some do and some do not. Continuation of this system of county-by-county decisions regarding how a dimpled chad is counted is fraught with equal protection concerns which will eventually cause the election results in Florida to be stricken by the federal courts or Congress.[25]

Said the Chief Justice: "My succinct conclusion is that the majority's decision to return this case to the circuit court for a count of the undervotes from either Miami-Dade or all counties has no foundation in the law of Florida as it existed on November 7, 2000, or at any time until the issuance of this opinion."[26]

Justice Harding, joined by Justice Shaw, concluded that the case came down to a failure of proof and an impossible remedy. "I would find that the selective recounting requested by Appellant is not available under the election contest provisions of section 102.168," wrote Justice Harding. "Such an application does not provide for a more accurate reflection of the will of the voters but rather, allows for an unfair distortion of the statewide vote."[27]

Indeed, Harding felt that Gore should not have been allowed to hand-pick counties during a contest period, first because he had won those counties and second because the contest challenges the results of an election and permitting Gore to raise issues only with a particular subset of counties is not probative of what a statewide recount would show. Yet even on his own terms, Gore had failed "to provide any meaningful statistical evidence that the outcome of the Florida election would be different if the 'no vote' in other counties had been counted; their proof that the outcome of the vote in two counties would likely change the results of the election was insufficient."[28]

Moreover, the court should not be in the position of ordering the lower court to perform tasks that are impossible to execute. All agreed that December 12 is the critical date. Harding wrote, "I am more concerned that the majority is departing from the essential requirement of the law by providing a remedy which is impossible to achieve and which will undoubtedly lead to chaos."[29]

At the Bush headquarters in Tallahassee, the mood had gone from building euphoria to shock and stunned disbelief. "It was worse than the first Florida Supreme Court decision," one Bush lawyer later recalled. "We thought Judge Sauls had given us several different ways to win. We thought his decision was bulletproof."

John Bolton found himself gasping for breath. "I felt like those Russian sailors on the *Kursk* must have felt," he remembered. "All you could do was stand by and feel your air run out."

Baker was bitter. To a colleague he remarked, "Florida is a state where the zombies don't stay dead."

There was no time for self-pity. Beck and his colleagues had to gather back at the circuit court, where Judge Sauls, angry and bitter, had recused himself from presiding over implementation of the state supreme court order and had been replaced by Judge Terry Lewis. Most of the 450 members of the field operations team, who had dispersed like dandelions in the breeze, had to be brought back to Tallahassee for midnight briefings and then flown to their assigned counties to represent Bush the following day. To beat Gore on the ground, the Bush team had to beat him on the logistics.

In addition, teams of brief-writers had to go back to work. The most critical task was to get the contest back to the U.S. Supreme Court before the count had gone too far. The state supreme court, by ordering that the 174 Palm Beach and 168 Miami-Dade numbers be included in the count, had narrowed Bush's lead to 195 votes. With tens of thousands of undervotes now subject to recount, Gore could move into the lead at any time, changing the entire dynamic of the contest. Baker, Olson, Terwilliger, and the other strategists knew that Bush must quickly ask the Court to stay the Florida recount and to treat the application for a stay as a request for certiorari.

There were also issues to get before Judge Lewis, suddenly presiding over his third major Florida recount case. The protest period had taught the Bush team the necessity of battling for the best results on the ground even while trying to preempt that battle in the courts. Their team met in preparation for the 8 A.M. session with Judge Lewis and decided to emphasize the need for strict counting standards and instant appeals by observers on the scene, safeguards they felt were essential to a fair process.

In practice, they would get nothing of the sort. Judge Lewis had ordered a team headed by David Leahy to begin counting the Miami-Dade undervotes at 8 A.M. Saturday in the Leon County Library. Two judges would be on hand to settle any disagreements. If they split, then Lewis himself would resolve the matter directly. As to the other counties, the canvassing boards were given until noon Saturday to organize themselves and convey their protocols to Lewis. Because of the leeway afforded trial judges to fashion remedies during the contest period, Lewis said he would not permit observers of either team to interrupt the counting process with objections, although they were free to take notes and argue their case with him at a later time.

Lewis would issue no guidance to the boards regarding the counting rules to be applied. Why not? "The supreme court has twice been given the opportunity and requested to give more specific criteria in terms of how to count ballots manually. They've declined to do so, and I'd see in that a clear indication that they'd wish to leave that to the canvassing boards and the persons that do the manual counting guided only by that principle that's laid out in the opinion."[30] That principle: determine the "clear intent" of the voter. Lewis would also order those engaged in the counting to provide no partial recount numbers to any party. Ron Klain, the senior Gore official on the scene, would routinely herald results from one county or another, claiming Gore was narrowing the gap minute by minute. His source of information, if any, remains a mystery to this day.

Beck, again representing Bush in a contest proceeding, was ready the following morning with a volley of legal shots at the revived count. Bush objected to the Lewis order on all the statutory and constitutional grounds he had been asserting since the opening effort to get the federal courts to halt the recount. The counting rules had been changed in midstream. The standardless counts violated the equal protection clause of the Fourteenth Amendment. Article 2 of the U.S. Constitution was being violated because the courts and not the legislature were making the law.

Now the Voting Rights Act of 1965 was also brought into play because of the state supreme court's bizarre endorsement of the 168-vote pick-up in Miami-Dade. There, only five of 199 predominantly Hispanic (mostly Cuban) precincts in the county had been included while African American and other pro-Gore constituencies had much higher percentage representation.

In one separate motion, Beck sought to exclude the "spoiled evidence" of the Miami-Dade ballots, because they had been degraded as county workers, with the delicacy of offensive linemen, sought to separate the undervotes. By now, Beck charged, they bore only scant relation to the ballots first counted on November 7. Beck also filed an emergency motion to take evidence on the "illegal votes" counted in Volusia and Broward counties due to the improvised permissive standards for counting dimpled chads. In fairness, his position here would have been stronger had he introduced evidence to that effect at the contest trial before Judge Sauls.

Lewis took the various Bush motions under advisement. In Washington, Olson, having filed the motion for a stay Friday night, gathered with colleagues to review the draft of a supplemental memorandum in support of the stay petition drafted by Cruz and Juster overnight. The memorandum pointed out a host of new legal and factual issues raised by Judge Lewis's ruling on how to conduct the recount. Throughout Saturday morning, it was truly a work in progress, changing and expanding as new information about the recount underway came to light.

Lewis took the various Bush moves under advisement. In Washington, Olson filed his motion for a stay. In Leon and most other counties across Florida, the counting began.

The resulting product, embracing both law and facts as fresh as the morning coffee, argued that the recount ordered by Judge Lewis was bound to produce chaos and injustice. The document included complaints about the following:

- The absence of statewide counting standards.

- The failure to ensure that counting would be conducted by impartial officials.

- The danger that some of the undervotes could be counted twice due to technical flaws in the process.

- The exclusion of three of the selective Gore counties and part of the fourth from the recount despite quirky and inconsistent counting techniques.

- The "bizarre" hybrid treatment afforded Miami-Dade County by the Florida Supreme Court, counting the Gore votes accumulated during the partial recount of heavily Democratic areas but only the undervotes in the remainder of the county, where Bush had won an Election Day majority.[31]

Ginsberg approved the memorandum, which was further massaged by Olson and his colleagues in Washington and filed with the U.S. Supreme Court. No one in Tallahassee could think of anything else to do. So they watched the manual recount proceed, and they waited for word from Washington.

CHAPTER **9**

Shutting the Door

For the Bush team, the first news Saturday was bracing: The recount nightmare was upon them, yet reports from the field suggested that their candidate was at least holding his own, even gaining a vote here and there. It was hard to put too much credence in the reports because a fair number of ballots were being contested by both sides, but there was a tinge of irony to Gore's developing predicament. Gore was being injured in the Florida election battle by friendly fire.

Tempering that good news was word that the 11th Circuit Court of Appeals in Atlanta, a body dominated by conservative jurists, had refused to come to the rescue, holding 8–4 that the recount could continue and denying Bush's request for an emergency hearing on the constitutionality of the manual recounts being conducted. However, the court had cushioned the blow, enjoining Florida officials from certifying any new results until the Supreme Court of the United States had accepted or rejected the opportunity for review.

Lawyers in Tallahassee who had worked on the U.S. Supreme Court brief or participated in the strategy surrounding it thought there was a good chance the Court would take the case, but they considered the chance of the Court staying the count no better than 50–50. For one thing, the burden of "proving irreparable" harm to support the stay was not easily shouldered. Bush had led wire to wire, and Lewis's order had barred the release of partial tallies. True the "spin-meisters" from both sides would be claiming big gains, but even if they had suddenly chugged gallons of truth serum, their estimates would be next to meaningless until ballot challenges, certainly to run into the hundreds if not thousands, were resolved. Also, as the most radical step the Court could take, a stay order would likely fracture the unanimity the Court had achieved in the counting deadline case handed down just days ago. In a constitutional issue of this sensitivity, the justices might still wish to speak with one voice. The High Court might well want to see how Judge Lewis handled the problem of diverse standards before tinkering with a stay order. Finally, any stay order would be far from procedural. It would almost certainly make it impossible for Florida to meet its deadline of December 12, even in the unlikely event that it later prevailed on appeal. For that reason, the lawyers thought that if the Court did order the counting stopped, it would almost be, in words shortly to be used by dissenting justices, "tantamount to a decision on the merits."

Shortly before 3 P.M., the stay order came down. The vote was 5–4 and both the majority and dissenters took the unusual step of venting their differences publicly. Dissenting were the four more-liberal members of the Court. Justice John Paul Stevens, writing for himself and Justices Souter, Ginsburg, and Breyer, argued that "counting every legally cast vote cannot constitute irreparable harm. On the other hand, there is a danger that a stay may cause irreparable harm to the respondents—and, more importantly, the public at large—because of the risk that 'the entry of the stay would be tantamount to a decision on the merits in favor of the applicants.'" The Florida court's ruling, said Stevens, "reflects the basic principle, inherent in our Constitution and our democracy, that every legal vote should be counted."[1]

While only four votes were needed for certiorari to be granted, the stay required a majority, and here one was provided by the five reliable conservatives, Chief Justice William H. Rehnquist and Justices O'Connor, Kennedy, Scalia, and Thomas. Responding to Stevens, Scalia wrote, "The counting of votes that are of questionable legality does in my view threaten irreparable harm to petitioner, and to the country, by casting a cloud upon what he claims to be the legitimacy of his election. Count first, and rule upon legality afterwards, is not a recipe for producing election results that have the public acceptance democratic stability requires." Further, said Scalia, the standards varying from county to county may well be unconstitutional. If it is, "permitting the count to proceed on that erroneous basis will prevent an accurate recount from being conducted on a proper basis later, since it is generally agreed that each manual recount produces a degradation of the ballots, which renders a subsequent recount inaccurate."

The majority vote to stay the count set off a cheer at GOP headquarters in Tallahassee. Knowing the historic import of the occasion, lawyers asked colleagues to sign their copies of the stay order. The event also triggered shocked cries of concern among Democrats. Boies, who had been as responsible as anyone for turning December 12 into the fail-safe date, conceded that there was now a "very serious issue" as to whether any procedure could be completed by that date even if the vice president managed to turn around a justice and prevail on the merits. Still he, like the Bush team, would pile the now familiar arguments into a brief required by 4 P.M. the following day and, by virtue of Gore's personal decision, replace Laurence Tribe at the oral argument on Monday morning. Chartered jets would take Evans, Rove, and the senior Bush lawyers to Washington for the argument, but Olson and the ubiquitous Joe Klock, still representing Katherine Harris, would present the case for the petitioners.

No sooner did Olson step forward to begin his presentation than he found himself on the defensive due to yet another inexplicable and shameless about-face engineered by the battery of Bush lawyers. Just as they had stunned the Florida Supreme Court by seeking to claim after oral argument that Florida's contest statute had no applicability to presidential elections, now they urged the U.S. Supreme Court that the Florida Supreme Court had been without jurisdiction to review the decision of the Florida circuit court where Judge Sauls had found on their behalf. Michael Carvin, who had worked on the brief, had advocated the position, but it had been rejected until after Chief Justice Wells raised it during the Florida Supreme Court argument.

"We were down to the wire and were not anxious to reject any argument that might possibly work," one Bush lawyer later recalled. "And because Chief Justice Wells in Florida had spent so much time suggesting a lack of jurisdiction, I guess someone figured, why not?" He might have added that so long as the Martin and Seminole County cases were before the Florida Second Circuit Court, no Bush lawyer in his right mind would have endorsed an argument against state supreme court review.

In fact, the election laws passed by the Florida legislature, which had plenary power over presidential selection in the state, bestowed enormous prerogatives on the circuit court, but made no mention of the state supreme court. Was the court simply assuming ordinary judicial review, as the Bush lawyers had suggested during the Florida Supreme Court argument? Or must the laws be interpreted literally and narrowly?

The naked Bush reversal impressed none of the justices, and when even O'Connor and Kennedy showed little patience with it, Olson was forced to concede, "It may not be the most powerful argument we bring to the Supreme Court."[2]

"I think that's right," replied Kennedy.

With this issue that never should have been before the Court wasting precious minutes of his time, Olson could only deal briefly with issues at the center of his case. One of the more vital ones was the importance of the December 12 deadline. As in the first Supreme Court argument, the issue was whether it was merely a "safe harbor" guideline for Congress, or whether it somehow assumed greater importance because it drew so much attention in the courts below.

Here Olson was able to make his point, telling Justice Souter, "Well, I believe that the Supreme Court of Florida certainly thought that it was construing—it certainly said so this time—that it was construing the applicability of Section 5 and it was expressing the hope that what it was doing was not jeopardizing the conclusive effect."[3]

That point was critical. If the Florida Supreme Court had effectively ruled that its solution to the contest was of no standing unless fully implemented by December 12, then Gore's case was constructively lost because the stay had already preempted the long-shot possibility that affairs could be settled by then.

The second critical issue grew out of what was clearly widely shared judicial concern about the Equal Protection argument. Yes, some of the Court liberals conceded, the different county standards raised that issue. But the Florida contest statute provides the presiding circuit court judge, now Terry Lewis, with the power "to fashion any order he or she deems necessary to prevent or correct any wrong, and to provide any relief appropriate under the circumstances."[4] Thus, in sorting out objections to the way the counties had recounted the votes, Judge Lewis could apply a uniform statewide standard. "I couldn't imagine a greater conferral of authority by the legislature to the circuit judge," Justice Ginsburg observed. That issue too would divide the conservative justices even from the liberals who recognized an equal protection problem with the Florida decision.

Olson was also able to get before the Justices an argument that, quirky and convoluted as it sounds, somehow would provide the five-justice majority with a way to keep the case from going back to the Florida Supreme Court in any meaningful sense and to justify that appropriation of state prerogative as an essential implementation of the will of the state. In a lengthy colloquy with Justice Souter, Olson found himself pushed to explain why the Court should be overly concerned about the ability of the state to meet a December 12 deadline upon remand when no such timetable or deadline is set forth in Section 168 of the Florida Election Code, the provision governing contests.

> **Olson:** It isn't just the timetable. The fact that there are timetables, which are very important in a presidential election, we are today smack up against a very important deadline and were in a process where . . .
>
> **Souter:** Yes, you are, but that is a deadline set by a safe harbor statute for the guidance of Congress and it's a deadline that has nothing to do with any text in 168.
>
> **Olson:** Well, I believe that the Supreme Court of Florida certainly thought that it was construing—it certainly said so this time—that it was construing the applicability of Section 5 and it was expressing the hope that what it was doing was not risking or jeopardizing the conclusive effect.[5]

Justice Souter then asked why, if the Bush people were so concerned with meeting the December 12 deadline, they sought a stay from the Supreme Court. Olson replied that with all the changes made in the election law through Florida Supreme Court decree, "that process had already violated Article 2 of the Constitution."

Justice Souter also drew a response from Olson that would go to the heart of the debate among justices who would agree that Florida procedures needed fixing to avert an equal protection problem, but who would disagree on the feasibility of trying to fix things at this late date. Asked by Souter what he thought would be a reasonable standard for counting undervotes, Olson replied that a starting point would be those with a complete puncture. Beyond that, he suggested that the secretary of state had the requisite expertise to determine which votes reflected voter intent sufficiently to be counted.

> **Souter:** If this were remanded to the Leon County Circuit Court, and the judge of that court addressed the secretary of state . . . and said, "Please tell us what the standard ought to be. We will be advised by your opinion," that would be feasible, wouldn't it?
>
> **Olson:** I think it would be feasible.[6]

Klock handled himself capably on the single issue of substance the justices chose to discuss with him: whether the

Florida Supreme Court had changed established Florida law, in effect legislating judicially, by declaring improperly executed ballots "legal votes" capable of triggering a recount rather than counting them incidental to a recount triggered by other, long-established causes, such as the malfunction of voting equipment. Klock pressed the latter interpretation with skill and command of the subject, but the later majority opinion, limited to equal protection, would ignore this issue. Rather, the question of change would find its way into the concurring opinion of three justices, led by Chief Justice Rehnquist, and the dissenting opinion filed by Justice Ginsburg.

Alas, Klock's time before the Court was made memorable by his sudden inability to distinguish one justice from another, not even the living from the dead:

Stevens: What standard would you use . . .
Klock: Well . . .
Stevens: . . . in the situation I proposed then?
Klock: Justice Brennan, the difficulty is that under—I'm sorry.
(Laughter)

And, moments later:

Klock: What I'm saying is . . .
Souter: They have to throw their hands up.
Klock: No, Justice Breyer. What I'm saying is . . .
Souter: I'm Justice Souter. You've got to cut that out.
(Laughter)

And, moments later:

Scalia: Mr. Klock? I'm Scalia.
(Laughter)
Klock: I'll remember that.
Scalia: Correct me if I'm wrong . . .
Klock: It will be hard to forget.[7]
(Laughter)

As the attorney seeking to defend what the Florida Supreme Court had done, Boies at times found himself a mere conduit

for scolding directed at the high-handedness of the state tribunal. Justice Kennedy, for example, got Boies to admit that
had the Florida legislature extended the protest period from
seven to nineteen days, it would have changed the law, thus
flouting federal law. Yet, Boies maintained, when the Florida
Supreme Court did the same thing, it was merely interpreting
rather than changing an existing law. Kennedy remained un-
convinced. "I'm not sure why if the legislature does it, it's a
new law, and when the supreme court does it, it isn't," he
grumbled.[8]

Justice O'Connor had her own peeves, two of them to be
precise. One was the fact that, without revising its earlier vacated decision, the state supreme court had essentially ignored
the U.S. Supreme Court's action by continuing to include in its
vote totals ballots that had been counted in Broward, Palm
Beach, and Miami-Dade Counties after the initial certification
date. "That's, I think, a concern that we have," she complained. "And I did not find, really, a response by the Florida
Supreme Court to this Court's remand in the case a week ago.
It just seemed to kind of bypass it and assume that all those
changes in deadlines were just fine, and they'd go ahead and
adhere to them. And I found that troublesome."[9]

Justice O'Connor seemed equally annoyed by the Florida
court's tortuous efforts to manipulate the state's protest and
contest periods to accommodate voters who had ignored
simple instructions on how to mark their ballots. "Well, why
isn't the standard the one that voters are instructed to follow,
for goodness' sake? I mean, it couldn't be clearer. I mean,
why don't we go to that standard?"[10]

Boies parried these questions as best he could, neither ad-
vancing his case nor suffering disaster. But when the argument finally turned to equal protection, the issue on which
the outcome of the case would turn, Boies seemed to lose the
invisible yet palpable advantage that had carried him
through two arguments in the Florida Supreme Court: the
notion that he was just a little bit smarter than anyone else
in the room.

His problem began when Justice Kennedy asked him whether, "from the standpoint of the equal protection clause, each—could each county give their own interpretation to what 'intent' means, so long as they are in good faith and with some reasonable basis for finding intent? Could that vary from county to county?"

"I think it can vary from individual to individual," Boies replied.[11] He compared the situation to a criminal trial or administrative practice hearing, where triers of fact may differ among themselves on who has satisfied what burden of proof. That wouldn't fly because, as Justice Kennedy promptly reminded him, "But here you have something objective. You're not just reading a person's mind; you're looking at a piece of paper."

Justice Souter leapt in. "Why shouldn't there be an objective rule for all counties?" he inquired. "And if there isn't, why isn't it an equal protection problem?"[12]

Here, the Bush lawyers sitting hushed in the courtroom feared, was a point where Boies could have offered a strong counterargument. It is not an equal protection problem because, for one thing, it does not work to the advantage or disadvantage of either candidate. Both are subject to identical standards within every county even if those standards differ from county to county. Second, no county is disadvantaged because each is free to adopt any reasonable standard it may wish for determining voter intent. Third, we are now at the stage where any material disparity creating unfairness can be reconciled by the single circuit court judge who must ultimately rule on every unresolved objection.

But Boies did not respond in anything like that fashion. Instead, in a stumbling retreat, he conceded that "maybe if you had specific objective criteria in one county that says we're going to count indented ballots, and another county that said we're only going to count the ballot if it's punched through, if you knew you had those two objective standards and they were different, then you might have an equal protection. . . ."

Justice Souter said, that being so, the Court would have to send the case back, "and I think we would have a responsibility to tell the Florida courts what to do about it. On that assumption, what would you tell them to do about it?"[13]

Boies: Well, I think that's a very hard question.
(Laughter)
Souter: You'd tell them to count every vote.
(Laughter)
Souter: You'd tell them to count every vote, Mr. Boies.
Boies: I'd tell them to count every vote.[14]
(Laughter)

Finally Justice Stevens came to Boies's rescue, asking, "Does not the procedure that is in place there contemplate that the uniformity will be achieved by having the final results all reviewed by the same judge?"

Boies took the life raft and agreed.

Scalia then jumped in, reminding Boies that the Florida Supreme Court had ordered election officials to accept the recounts from both Broward and Palm Beach Counties despite the differing standards.

Boies corrected Scalia, noting that Broward had been certified and was not at issue at the time of the second Florida Supreme Court decision and that Palm Beach and Miami-Dade were the two counties involved.

Boies continued: "And, with respect to Miami-Dade and Palm Beach, I do not believe that there is evidence in the record that that is a different standard. And there's no finding of the trial court that that was a different standard. Indeed, what the trial court found was that both Miami-Dade and Palm Beach properly exercised their counting responsibilities."[15]

This response stretched the truth. True, the Palm Beach County recount had been approved by Judge Sauls, but Miami-Dade's liberal method was before the court only as an example of ballots degraded by careless counting practices. The "counting responsibilities" endorsed by Judge Sauls in-

volved the canvassing board's decision to *stop* counting because of an inability to meet the deadline, not, as Boies suggested, approval of the standards used in counting the votes.

Boies also misled the Court during further discussion with
Scalia about the decision by the Florida Supreme Court to
include in Gore's total the votes of Broward County recounted in a procedure ordered by the Florida Supreme
Court but vacated on December 4 by the U.S. Supreme
Court. "I think what the Supreme Court is saying is you've
got a certification," said Boies. "That certification shows a
certain vote total. Now, you take that certification until it is
contested, and it can be contested by either or both parties.
You do not have, until it is contested, you do not have contested ballots."[16] Certainly when he made that statement,
Boies knew that under Florida law, only the loser, not "either
or both parties," can bring an election contest lawsuit.

The Court briefly visited the omission of overvotes—ballots
disqualified because at least two votes were punched for the
presidency. They exceeded twice the number of remaining undervotes, but generally raised fewer questions of interpretation. The Bush brief noted, however, that a voter punching
"write-in" and George W. Bush would have his vote disqualified, though he might well have written in for Bush, thus
making clear his intent. The issue was unlikely to prove de-
terminative, but a sympathetic justice seeking to marshal
every argument he could might well have referred to it.

Boies made one fleeting effort to salvage his position by
reminding the court that differences in voting equipment
have a more profound impact on the number of voter errors
than do differences in counting methods. Justice O'Connor
presented the issue to Olson during his rebuttal argument.
"How can you have one standard when there are so many
varieties of ballots?" she asked.

This time Olson's response was crisp and precise: "Certainly the standard should be that similarly situated voters
and similarly situated ballots ought to be evaluated by comparable standards."[17]

Moments later, the Chief Justice announced, "This case is submitted," and the courtroom emptied. Later in the day, the Florida Supreme Court issued a revised opinion in the first *Gore v. Harris* case, reaching the identical result on extending the certification deadline from November 14 to November 26, but purporting to do so purely on the basis of statutory law.

Belying profound differences in philosophy and assessment of the law, the Florida House and Senate now moved in lockstep toward the appointment of the same slate of Bush electors that had been chosen prior to the November 7 election. Committees of both the House and Senate passed joint resolutions to that effect on December 11, balking at a legislative bill in order to save time and avert a gubernatorial signature, which they feared would have compromised their plenary power in this area.

The House planned to vote on the resolution the following day, the Senate later in the week. For House Speaker Tom Feeney, a hard-charging, highly intelligent conservative activist from Pennsylvania, the moment was sweet. Still smarting from past state supreme court rebuffs—that court had declared two of his most important criminal law reform bills unconstitutional and had kept some of his pet antitax initiatives off the ballot—Feeney now felt they were playing on his home court. "I felt that after the Florida Supreme Court changed the law by extending the protest period, that any count as a result of that was fabrication and extra-constitutional and was meaningless," he later recalled. "Don Rubottom and my other legal advisers told me we could have acted any time after they changed the law. I also felt they acted illegally in stopping the secretary of state from exercising her discretion under the law. Her guidelines were reasonable. The court mistakenly invoked its so-called equitable powers to overturn what it called her 'hypertechnical' enforcement of the law."

If Feeney had his way, the legislature would have taken matters in hand early on. "We didn't see a constitutional problem acting after the twelfth," he recalled, "but we wanted to move fast because we didn't want to wake up to see a headline saying, 'Gore ahead by 5,000 votes.' The way we ended up doing it gave us a lot more cover on TV. It would have been a dramatically different situation had Gore taken the lead."

Feeney had been among the Florida Republicans urging Bush to resist a statewide recount at all costs. "We thought we might get hurt," he recalled. "For example, Bush won Duvall County, but our experts said the undercounted ballots had been disproportionately in Democratic precincts."

Feeney's Senate counterpart was the cautious, courtly, and collegial John McKay. While the two men get along reasonably well, they could hardly be more opposite. Feeney jogs to stay lean and mean for his legislative donnybrooks; McKay golfs because he worships the game and believes that any difference that can't be worked out by the fourth hole probably is insoluble.

McKay believed that the Florida Supreme Court, by legislating from the bench, had placed the state's electoral college votes in jeopardy and that, unless the dispute was settled by December 12, six million Floridians could have been disenfranchised. "My primary responsibility was not to Bush, the Republican Party, or the Senate," he later recalled. "It was to Florida. I would have elected a slate of Gore delegates had that been in Florida's interest."

McKay's in-house counsel, Steve Kahn, took a cautious approach. There was no legal basis for the legislature to move prior to December 12, he concluded. "Steve felt that was dropping the checkered flag," McKay recalled. "He also felt the eighteenth, when the states met to cast their ballots, was the really important date. If the Florida combatants could resolve their dispute by that date, the safe harbor provisions of federal law would be irrelevant because there would be no slates competing with the one to emerge from the lengthy battle."

Despite bravado, no one in the Bush camp felt particularly sanguine about relying on the Florida legislature to determine the next president. What would happen if the legislature moved on the twelfth or thirteenth to appoint a slate of Bush electors and on the sixteenth a completed recount had Gore in the lead? Suppose the state supreme court sanctioned the result with Gore in the lead and issued a writ of mandamus commanding the governor to sign that result and forward it to the National Archives, the repository for election documents? The legislature was given power to determine presidential elections in Florida, but it would certainly be argued that the legislature had exercised that power by setting up the Election Day vote plus the series of protest, contest, and appellate procedures now in full movement.

Federal law was not much help. It provided that the electors of each state meet "on the first Monday after the second Wednesday in December," which fell on December 1 in the year 2000, to determine that state's vote for president and vice president. But it is not until January 6 when Congress counts the electoral votes. If there are competing slates from a particular state, the two Houses of Congress meet separately to decide which one is entitled to be counted. If they disagree, "the votes of the electors whose appointment shall have been certified by the executive of the State, under the seal thereof, shall be counted."[18] But was the Governor of Florida, Jeb Bush, an independent actor in this process? Or was his role purely ministerial, to be determined ultimately by one supreme court or another?

On January 6, 2001, Republicans would control the U.S. House, with the Senate split 50–50, tie votes to be broken by Vice President Albert Gore. Should Gore pull ahead in the Florida popular vote, how would George W. Bush look, trailing Al Gore by nearly half a million popular votes nationally, seeking to be imposed on the country by a resolution of the Florida legislature?

"We would never have done that, I'll tell you that," James Baker later recalled. "That's not the way George W. Bush wanted to be president. It was great having the Florida legislature in our corner. But we needed to win in the Supreme Court."

Late in the evening of December 12, the Supreme Court of the United States effectively ended the battle for the White House by holding that the recount ordered by the Florida Supreme Court violated the principle of equal protection by subjecting ballots in different counties to widely divergent counting rules and that the effort by the Florida Supreme Court to resolve all disputes by December 12 reflected the will of the legislature, had the force of law, and was under the circumstances impossible to achieve. The unsigned decision was by a 5–4 vote reflecting the liberal-conservative court split. Two of the liberal justices, Souter and Breyer, agreed that equal protection was a serious problem, but each would have sent the case back to Florida and permitted the state to try to salvage the situation by the time the electoral college met on December 18. Chief Justice Rehnquist, joined by Justices Scalia and Thomas, would have included as additional grounds for reversal actions by the Florida court that, they argued, made new law, usurping the functions of the state legislature in violation of Article 2 of the Constitution.

Endorsing the right to vote as "fundamental," the majority concluded, "The recount mechanisms implemented in response to the decisions of the Florida supreme court do not satisfy the minimum requirement for non-arbitrary treatment of voters necessary to secure the fundamental right."[19]

Borrowing heavily from the supplemental Bush brief on the stay petition, the court relied on documented examples of divergent standards applied and even of changes within particular counties. For example, "Broward County used a more forgiving standard than Palm Beach County, and uncovered almost three times as many new votes, a result markedly disproportionate to the difference in population between the counties."[20]

The court also found no valid excuse for ignoring overvotes, given the fact that there were up to 110,000 of them to be left unexamined under the state court ruling while attention was lavished on the roughly 60,000 undervotes.

The Florida court's effort to count the Miami-Dade partial vote from the overwhelmingly Gore precincts drew one of the U.S. Supreme Court's most pointed rebukes. "This accommodation no doubt results from the truncated contest period established by the Florida Supreme Court in *Bush 1*, at respondent's own urging. The press of time does not diminish the constitutional concern. A desire for speed is not a general excuse for ignoring equal protection guarantees."[21]

Returning to the material in the supplemental brief, the court found even the latest state court order pregnant with constitutional concerns. "That order did not specify who would recount the ballots. . . . Further, while others were permitted to observe, they were prohibited from objecting during the recount."[22]

At issue, said the majority, was not the right of local entities to develop different systems for conducting elections. "Instead, we are presented with a situation where a state court with the power to assure uniformity has ordered a statewide recount with minimal procedural safeguards. When a court orders a statewide remedy, there must be at least some assurance that the rudimentary requirements of equal treatment and fundamental fairness are satisfied."[23]

Noting that any remand for further counting would require both the adoption of new procedures plus later judicial review to resolve disputes, the Court concluded that, "Because it is evident that any recount seeking to meet the December 12 date will be unconstitutional for the reasons we have discussed, we reverse the judgment of the Supreme Court of Florida ordering a recount to proceed."[24]

The dissent, commanding support from all four in the minority, was written by Justice Stevens. He described the equal protection argument as "not substantial." Admittedly, the use of different standards from county to county "may raise serious concerns." But, "Those concerns are alleviated—if not eliminated—by the fact that a single impartial magistrate will ultimately adjudicate all objections arising from the recount process."[25]

Stevens said that underlying the "entire federal assault on the Florida election procedures is an unstated lack of confidence in the impartiality and capacity of the state judges who would make the critical decisions if the vote count were to proceed," and that "can only lend credence to the most cynical appraisal of the work of judges throughout the land." And while we may never know the real winner of this year's election, said Stevens, the certain loser "is the nation's confidence in the judge as an impartial guardian of the rule of law."

Justices Souter and Breyer, in separate dissents, endorsed the equal protection conclusion of the majority, but urged a remedy that would have given the state the opportunity to correct the flaws and decide for itself whether the December 12 date was critical.

Noting that electoral votes were scheduled to be cast in six days, Souter would have remanded the case to the courts of Florida "with instructions to establish uniform standards for evaluating the several types of ballots that have prompted differing treatments."[26]

Breyer would have remanded the case with instructions to count all undercounted votes, including those in Broward, Miami-Dade, Palm Beach, and Volusia—Gore's handpicked counties—"and to do so in accordance with a single uniform standard."[27] Somewhat inconsistently, Breyer criticized the Court for "improvidently" stopping a recount the state might have completed in time to meet its deadline. Exactly why an unconstitutional recount should have proceeded, he did not explain.

It is difficult to imagine why Justices Kennedy and O'Connor declined to join Chief Justice Rehnquist's opinion, particularly given their statements from the bench during oral argument. Perhaps they wanted to hold a clear majority of seven justices behind the Court's assessment of the constitutional wrong even if two of their brethren could not endorse the remedy. In doing so, they left many to wonder whether stopping the process cold was really necessary. Why not, as Breyer and Souter had suggested, leave it to Florida to see if it could complete a process in the time allotted by both the federal government and its own legislature?

By contrast, Rehnquist hammered at the pattern of judicial excesses committed by the Florida court. "This inquiry does not imply a disrespect for state *courts*," wrote the Chief Justice, "but rather a respect for the constitutionally prescribed role of state *legislatures*."[28] His attack on constitutional infirmities—violations of Article 2—was substantial

After extending the certification deadline and "shortchanging the contest period," the state court implied that "certification was a matter of significance" with the winner enjoying "presumptive validity" and the loser facing "an uphill battle. In its latest opinion, however, the court empties certification of virtually all legal consequence,"[29] thereby departing from the legislative scheme.

"No reasonable person would call it 'an error in the vote tabulation,'" Rehnquist continued, "or a 'rejection of legal votes,' when electronic or electromechanical equipment performs precisely in the manner designed, and fails to count those ballots that are not marked in the manner that these voting instructions explicitly and prominently specify."[30] And when the secretary of state "rejected this peculiar reading of the statutes" and offered a reasonable one, the state court struck her action down.

Thus, in the view of the Chief Justice and those who concurred with him, the Florida Supreme Court had tainted the process to the point where it could not be fixed. By contrast, the majority opinion concluded that those constitutional infirmities on which the decision hinged were curable, but they could not be cured in the allotted time.

At Bush headquarters in Tallahassee, there was simply no work to be done while they awaited the Supreme Court decision. Lawyers tossed footballs in the yard and on the street. In some cases, clients or partners received unexpected phone calls from men (mostly) who had been off in their own world for the past month. Day turned into evening and evening into night with no word. When the decision did come down, Don Evans happened to be on the phone with George W. Bush. "I gotta call you back, buddy," he said, hanging up. As network correspondents struggled to interpret the ruling in Washington, the lawyers in Tallahassee were doing the same, as were the people around the governor of Texas.

Then the phone rang. It was Governor Bush looking for James Baker.

"Good evening, Mr. President-elect," said Baker, and a huge cheer erupted. Baker said he planned a low-key reaction. He didn't want to smear egg on the face of Gore's lawyers.

Then Evans's cell phone rang. Dick Cheney was on the other end wanting to speak to Baker.

"It's Big Time," announced Evans. Cheney had earned that nickname on the campaign trail after Bush had referred to a *New York Times* reporter as an "asshole" and Cheney had dutifully replied, "Big time."

"Jim," said Cheney. "Congratulations. Only under your leadership could we have gone from a lead of 1,800 votes to a lead of 150 votes."

John Bolton, who had run the ground war in Palm Beach County, observed the scene. He never much liked Gore, and thought Bush might save the country from the Clinton epoch of moral and political permissiveness. Nonetheless, he wished it all could have happened without a U.S. Supreme Court decision imposing ad hoc constitutional standards on the states. Bolton also had a dispassionate sense of the grand stroke of luck that had made it all end so well.

"If the canvassing board had been two partisan Democrats or three partisan Democrats in Palm Beach County, we'd have been screwed," he later said.

Among the Bush lawyers who waged the battle in Florida, few would join Bolton in complaining about the route traveled by the U.S. Supreme Court in reaching its conclusion. Mentally, most seemed still to be combatants in the battle of recounts, trading jabs with protagonists, arguing fiercely for positions long since determined, seeing little distinction between the instant verdict and that of history.

Among those capable of more detached reflection, two themes seemed dominant: First, a feeling of professional pride and accomplishment in what they had achieved. Gore, starting the battle with a ferocious head of steam had been neutralized and then defeated on every front . . . before the canvassing boards, in the courts, and ultimately, in the political arena. And it had not happened by chance, but rather by decisions as to where and how to fight and not to fight, and by the strategic deployment of human resources.

The second theme was an overwhelming sense that the rogue player in the battle was not Al Gore or Joseph Lieberman, not William Daley and Warren Christopher, and not even David Boies, but the Florida Supreme Court. These justices, particularly the four that constituted the majority in the appeal from the contest trial decision of Judge Sanders Sauls, were the perpetrators of the constitutional crisis of Election 2000. This was the body that was totally out of control. These were the justices that:

• Transformed voter error into an "error on vote tabulation" sufficient to warrant a recount.

• Turned the statutory discretion of the Secretary of State to reject recounts not meeting the seven-day deadline into a prohibition against rejecting any late recount so long as it does not impede the contest period.

• Legislated new deadline dates from the bench.

• Failed to adhere to its own deadlines.

• Failed to hold counties to a consistent recount standard.

• Allowed Gore to keep a 168-vote pickup in Miami-Dade County despite the fact that the recount had been limited to staunch Democratic precincts.

• Gave negligible weight to canvassing board decisions made during the protest period.

- Set a statistically banal standard to justify contest period recounts, saying one should be ordered whenever the number of undervotes exceeds the margin between the top two candidates.

- Ignored the first Supreme Court decision until after the second appeal was argued, thereby insulting the U.S. Supreme Court and angering at least one of its justices.

A tendency to intrude on the discretion of states exercising their sovereign functions is far from the most prominent instinct of the current U.S. Supreme Court. But when confronted with lawless frolic by a supreme state tribunal in an enterprise of monumental national significance, the court found intervention imperative. And it was the work of James Baker and his colleagues in Tallahassee that defined the essence of the controversy and determined the forum for its resolution.

In the months ahead, political opponents would snipe at the results, hoping to cripple the infant Bush presidency. Their efforts would come to naught, in part because Mr. Bush outlined and then pursued his agenda with the apparent confidence of a man who had achieved a victory of landslide proportions. The critics also lacked a guiding voice, Al Gore having gracefully recused himself to grow a beard and a belly while the Bush presidency took hold. Future historians may well spend years pouring over the nuances of the Florida contest, but they will likely conclude that those who fought that contest quickly moved on.

Postscript

On December 22, the Florida Supreme Court issued its third and final opinion in *Gore v. Harris*. It was about as widely anticipated as a July 5 confetti sale. Gore had long since conceded, George W. Bush had captured 271 votes when the electoral college met on December 18, and Congress was preparing a pro forma electoral vote-counting session on January 6 with the vice president presiding.

In a three-page per curium opinion, the Florida Supreme Court concluded that the U.S. Supreme Court had pretty well put them out of business. Not only could the December 12 deadline not have been met, but the court should not be the party seeking to devise counting standards to pass constitutional muster: "Moreover, upon reflection, we conclude that the development of a specific, uniform standard necessary to ensure equal application and to secure the fundamental right to vote throughout the State of Florida should be left to the body we believe best equipped to study and address it, the Legislature."[1]

Having the two most important cases any of these jurists will ever sit on vacated by the United States Supreme Court was downright humbling.

Justice Leander J. Shaw's concurring opinion deserves to be noted. While he dissented from the court's December 8 decision, he remained bothered by the way in which the December 12 date had been adopted as the deadline for resolving matters in Florida:

> First, in my opinion, December 12 was not a drop-dead date under Florida law. In fact, I question whether any date prior to January 6 is a drop-dead date under the Florida election scheme. December 12 was simply a *permissive* safe-harbor date to which the states could aspire. It certainly was not a *mandatory* contest deadline under the plain language of the Florida Election Code (i.e., it is not mentioned there) or this Court's prior rulings.[2]

Justice Shaw would seem to be absolutely right. December 12 was simply a target of opportunity for Gore's chief lawyer, David Boies, to point to when he was trying to make his man a winner by collecting all those lovely dimples in those four selected counties. To use one of the hoariest yet most telling metaphors in the law, Mr. Boies was hoisted on his own petard.

Notes

Chapter 1

1. Federal Document Clearing House, Gore and Lieberman in Washington, Nov. 8, 2000, p. 2.
2. Federal Document Clearing House, Daley in Washington, Nov. 8, 2000, p. 5.
3. Federal Document Clearing House, Daley in Florida, Nov. 10, 2000, p. 2.
4. eMediaMillWorks, Inc., Nov. 9, 2000, p. 1.
5. *Nelson v. Robinson*, 2d Dist. Fla. Ct. of App., No. 74-1201, Oct. 15, 1974.
6. eMediaMillWorks, Inc., Dan Evans Holds News Conference on Florida Recount, Nov. 9, 2000, p. 3.
7. "Are Chads Democrats? An Analysis of the Florida Presidential Recount," Dec. 2, 2000, unpublished, p. 2.
8. Ibid., p. 10.
9. Transcript, Christopher/Daley Presser, Naval Observatory, Washington, D.C., Nov. 11, 2000, p. 3.
10. *The Recount Primer*, Timothy Downs, Chris Sauter, John Hardin Young, self-published, Aug., 1994, p. 5.
11. Ibid., p. 5.
12. Absolute discretion for canvassing boards, § 102.166(4)(c).
13. Error in voter tabulation, § 102.166(5).

Chapter 2

1. *36 Days: The Complete Chronicle of the 2000 Presidential Election Crisis,* Times Books, 2001, p. 29.
2. Federal Document Clearing House, George W. Bush, Nov. 10, 2000, p. 1.
3. Text released by Baker, Nov. 11, 2000, p. 1.
4. eMediaMillWorks, Inc., Daley/Christopher Presser, Nov. 11, 2000, p. 2.
5. eMediaMillWorks, Inc., Baker in Florida, Nov. 11, 2000, p. 3.
6. Statute 3, U.S.C. § 5.
7. *Siegel v. LePore,* U.S.D.C. Southern District, Florida, No. 00-9007, slip op., Nov. 13, 2000, p. 18.
8. *36 Days,* pp. 113–114.
9. Harris, letter to Al Cardenas, Nov. 13, 2000, p. 2.
10. Attorney General Robert A. Butterworth, letter to Judge Charles E. Burton, Nov. 14, 2000, p. 1.
11. Advisory Legal Opinion to Judge Burton, Nov. 14, 2000.
12. Florida deadline statute, § 102.111, § 102.112.
13. Federal Document Clearing House, Daley/Christopher Presser, Nov. 15, 2000, p. 2.
14. *Gore v. Harris,* 2d Jud. Cir. Ct., Leon County, Case No. 00-2700, slip op., Nov. 14, 2000, pp. 2–3.
15. Ibid., p. 6.
16. *36 Days,* p. 76.
17. Federal Document Clearing House, Harris in Tallahassee, Nov. 15, 2000.
18. *36 Days,* p. 78.
19. *36 Days,* p. 86.
20. *Gore v. Harris, supra,* p. 2.

Chapter 3

1. *Palm Beach County Canvassing Board v. Harris,* Sup. Ct. Fla., No. SCOO-2431, Brief of Appellants, pp. 6–7.
2. *Palm Beach County Canvassing Board v. Harris,* Amended Brief of Appellees, pp. 43–44.
3. *Roudebush v. Hartke,* 405 U.S. 15, (1972).
4. Fla. Sup. Ct. Broadcast Archives. Oral Argument Transcript: Presidential Election Cases, Nov. 20, 2000, p. 4.
5. Ibid., p. 10.
6. Ibid., pp. 10–12.
7. Ibid., p. 11.
8. Ibid., p. 14.
9. Ibid., p. 23.

10. *Broward County Canvassing Board v. Hogan*, Fla. Sup. Ct., 607 So.2d 508, (1992).
11. Broadcast Archives, p. 22.
12. Ibid., p. 23.
13. Ibid., p. 28.
14. Ibid., p. 32.
15. Ibid., p. 36.
16. Ibid., p. 37.
17. *Palm Beach County Canvassing Board v. Harris*, Nov. 21, 2000, slip op., p. 36.
18. opinion, Ibid., p. 39.
19. opinion, Ibid., pp. 39-40.
20. *Pullen v. Mulligan*, Ill. Sup. Ct. 38 Ill.2d 21, (1990).
21. Text of Baker statement, Nov. 21, 2000.

Chapter 4

1. The Associated Press, Nov. 11, 2000.
2. *The New York Times*, Nov. 13, 2000, p. A26.
3. *Newsday*, Nov. 13, 2000, A17.
4. Nov. 15 County Canvassing Board Hearing Transcript, p. 35. *Miami Herald*, Nov. 24, 2000, p. 1.
5. *Delahunt v. Johnson*, 423 Mass. 731, (1996).
6. *The Washington Post*, Nov. 24, 2000, p. A01.
7. *The New York Times*, Nov. 21, 2000, p. A21.
8. *36 Days*, p. 103.
9. *Miami Herald*, Nov. 22, 17A.
10. *Miami Herald*, Nov. 21, 17A.
11. *36 Days*, p. 120.
12. *The New York Times*, Nov. 24, 2000, p. A40.
13. *36 Days*, p. 135.
14. Press Conference, Nov. 15, 2000.
15. *Florida Democratic Party v. Palm Beach County Canvassing Board*, Palm Beach County Cir. Ct., No. CL 00-11078 AB, Declaratory Order, Nov. 15, 2000.
16. *Gore v. Harris*, 2d Jud. Ct., Leon County Civil Division, No. 00-2808, Transcript of Contest Hearing, Dec. 2, 2000, p. 258.
17. *Florida Democratic Party v. Palm Beach County Canvassing Board*, Order on Plaintiff's Emergency Motion to Clarify Declaratory Order of November 15, 2000, Nov. 22, 2000.
18. Consent Decree, *United States of America v. Florida*, Civ. Action No. TCA-80 1055, U.S.D.C., Northern District of Florida, Aug. 20, 1982.
19. Herron Memo, Nov. 15, 2000, pp. 1–2.

20. A compilation of county by county absentee ballot disqualifications appears as Exhibit 7 in the Appendix to Plaintiff's Memorandum in Support of Complaint for Declaratory Relief, *Bush v. Hillsborough County Canvassing Board*, U.S.D.C., Northern District, Florida, No. 300-533-LAC.
21. *36 Days*, p. 101.
22. Meet The Press, Nov. 19, 2000.
23. Letter to all county supervisors of elections and all county canvassing boards, Nov. 20, 2000.
24. Judge Lace A. Collier Declaratory Judgment, *Bush v. Hillsborough County Canvassing Board*, p. 28.
25. Rejected draft of Bush speech made available to author.
26. *36 Days*, p. 167.
27. Text of Baker statement provided by Baker.

Chapter 5

1. 3 U.S.C. § 5, Order List, Friday Nov. 27, 2000, *Bush v. Palm Beach County Canvassing Board*, 531 U.S., No. 00-836.
2. A copy of the Option Memo was made available to the author.
3. *Bush v. Palm Beach County Canvassing Board*, U.S. Sup. Ct., Brief for Petitioner, No. 00-836, pp. 13–14.
4. The Associated Press Transcript of Oral Argument, Dec. 1, 2000, p. 20.
5. *Bush v. Palm Beach County Canvassing Board*, U.S. Sup. Ct., p. 15.
6. Ibid., p. 35.
7. Ibid., p. 40.
8. Ibid., p. 63.
9. Ibid., p. 61.
10. Ibid., p. 60.
11. *Bush v. Palm Beach County Canvassing Board*, 121 U.S. Sup. Ct. 471 (2000), p. 475.

Chapter 6

1. *36 Days*, pp. 55–56.
2. *Boardman v. Esteva*, 323 So.2d 265, (1975).
3. *Beckstrom v. Volusia County Canvassing Board*, 701 So.2d 720, (1998).
4. *Washington Post*, Feb. 1, 2000, p. A1.
5. Federal Document Clearing House, Gore at the White House, Dec. 5, 2000, p. 2.
6. *Jacobs v. The Seminole County Canvassing Board*, 2d Jud. Cir. for Leon County, Florida, slip op., Dec. 8, 2000.

7. Ibid., p. 10.
8. *Taylor v. The Martin County Canvassing Board*, 2d Cir. Ct., slip op. at 8, N00-2850, Dec. 8, 2000.

Chapter 7

1. Reuters Script Wires, Boies/Douglas/Hattaway Presser at Florida State Capitol, Nov. 26, 2000, pp. 1–2.
2. Ibid., pp. 2–3.
3. Ibid., p. 5.
4. *Gore v. Harris*, No. 0038, 2d Cir. Ct. for the Jud. Cir. Leon County Florida, (contest transcript), pp. 4, 6.
5. Ibid., p. 6.
6. Ibid., p. 12.
7. Ibid., pp. 17–20.
8. Ibid., pp. 110–111.
9. Ibid., p. 129.
10. Ibid., p. 190.
11. Ibid., p. 258.
12. Ibid., p. 284.
13. Ibid., pp. 326–327.
14. Ibid., pp. 337–338.
15. Ibid., p. 405.
16. Ibid., p. 411.
17. Ibid., p. 420.
18. Ibid., pp. 437–438.
19. Ibid., p. 442.
20. Ibid., pp. 505–506.
21. Ibid., p. 521.
22. Ibid., p. 719.
23. eMediaMillWorks, Inc., text of Judge N. Saul Sanders Decision, Dec. 4, 2000, p. 1.
24. Ibid., p. 2.
25. *36 Days,* p. 236.
26. *Chicago Tribune*, Dec. 5, 2000, p. A1.

Chapter 8

1. *Gore v. Harris,* Sup. Ct. Fla., No. SCOO-2431. eMediaMillWorks, Inc., text of Fla. Sup. Ct. Arguments, Dec. 7, 2000, pp. 5–6.
2. Ibid., p. 6.
3. Ibid., p. 8.
4. Ibid., p. 11.
5. Ibid., p. 18.

6. Ibid., p. 18.
7. Ibid., p. 18.
8. Ibid., p. 21.
9. Ibid., p. 24.
10. Ibid., p. 26.
11. *Gore v. Harris,* slip op., Dec. 8, 2000, footnote 7, p. 6.
12. Brief, Boies press availability, Dec. 8, 2000.
13. opinion, p. 33.
14. Ibid., p. 16.
15. Ibid., pp. 22–23.
16. Ibid., p. 25.
17. Ibid., p. 31.
18. *Gore v. Harris,* No. 0038, 2d Cir. Ct. for the Jud. Cir. Leon County, Fla., (contest), transcript, p. 278.
19. opinion, p. 34.
20. Ibid., p. 30.
21. Ibid., footnote 21, p. 38.
22. Ibid., p. 41.
23. Ibid., pp. 49–50.
24. Ibid., pp. 52–53.
25. Ibid., pp. 51–52.
26. Ibid., p. 41.
27. Ibid., p. 66.
28. Ibid., p. 65.
29. Ibid., p. 67.
30. Baker Botts transcript from tape, p. 5.
31. *Bush v. Gore,* Supplemental Memorandum, pp. 2–5.

Chapter 9

1. *Bush v. Gore,* No. 00-949, issued Dec. 9, 2000, *36 Days,* pp. 281–283.
2. CNN oral argument transcript, Dec. 11, 2000, p. 5.
3. Ibid., p. 8.
4. Ibid., p. 11.
5. Ibid., p. 8.
6. Ibid., pp. 10–11.
7. Ibid., pp. 17–18.
8. Ibid., p. 21.
9. Ibid., p. 27.
10. Ibid., p. 31.
11. Ibid., pp. 23–24.
12. Ibid., p. 24.

13. Ibid., p. 25.
14. Ibid., p. 25.
15. Ibid., p. 26.
16. Ibid., p. 32.
17. Ibid., p. 39.
18. Federal laws on counting electoral votes, 3 U.S.C. § 15.
19. *Bush v. Gore,* 121 Sup. Ct. 525 (2000), p. 530.
20. Ibid., p. 531.
21. Ibid., p. 532.
22. Ibid., p. 532.
23. Ibid., p. 532.
24. Ibid., p. 533.
25. Ibid., p. 541.
26. Ibid., p. 545.
27. Ibid., p. 551.
28. Ibid., p. 535.
29. Ibid., pp. 536–537.
30. Ibid., p. 537.

Postscript

1. *Gore v. Harris*, No. S000-4431, Fla. Sup. Ct., Dec. 22, 2000, slip op., p. 2.
2. Ibid., p. 8.

Index